Letters to Gorbachev

Ron McKay is a journalist who has worked for the BBC, national and local papers and *Campaign* for whom he wrote a weekly column. He has travelled extensively, interviewing among others Arafat and Gadaffi. The idea for *Letters to Gorbachev* was a joint project conceived by Ron McKay and the editor of *Argumenty i Fakty*.

LETTERS TO GORBACHEV

Life in Russia Through the Postbag of
Argumenty i Fakty

Edited by
Ron McKay

Michael Joseph
LONDON

MICHAEL JOSEPH LTD

Published by the Penguin Group
Penguin Books Ltd, 27 Wrights Lane, London W8 5TZ, England
Viking Penguin, a division of Penguin Books USA Inc.
375 Hudson Street, New York, New York 10014, USA
Penguin Books Australia Ltd, Ringwood, Victoria, Australia
Penguin Books Canada Ltd, 2801 John Street, Markham, Ontario, Canada L3R 1B4
Penguin Books (NZ) Ltd, 182–190 Wairau Road, Auckland 10, New Zealand

Penguin Books Ltd, Registered Offices: Harmondsworth, Middlesex, England

First published in Great Britain 1991

Typeset in 11 on 12½ pt. Photina, printed and bound in
England by Clays Ltd, St Ives plc

A CIP catalogue record for this book is available from the British Library

ISBN 0 7181 3498 2

Svetlana Egorova heads AIF's letters department and with her team orders, grades and makes sense of the tens of thousands of letters the newspaper receives each week. This book wouldn't have been possible without her.

It is dedicated to my friend Olga Bogatova, Hollywood's greatest loss, whose eminent good sense, warm company and home baking made me completely at home on my visits to Moscow.

Ludmilla Makarova expertly translated many of the letters and she and her family Lucy, Sasha and Masha virtually adopted me.

Not forgetting the Do Svedanya Pets at the National, Lindsay, Davie, Jack, Keith and crew.

CONTENTS

'The President receives many letters from individual citizens and public organizations requesting him to introduce presidential rule to ward off tragedies and to prevent their escalation. But no such requests have ever come from local authorities. What's the matter? Where are they? What is their position? As a result attempts are being made to shift the entire blame on to the President.' – **Mikhail Gorbachev.**

'It is easy to see that the centre is doing everything it can in order to frustrate the efforts to consolidate the economic foundations of our sovereignty ... The centre interferes in the republic's ethnic affairs. We are experiencing enormous difficulties in obtaining foreign credits and aid. Does not the Ryzhkov government understand that their policy hits ordinary people the hardest? Clearly the will of the 150 million citizens of the Russian Federation can be disregarded only with the approval and support of the country's supreme leadership.' – **Boris Yeltsin.**

PREFACE

Dear Readers,

This is a book of letters received by *Argumenty i Fakty*, the largest publication in the world. We're in the *Guinness Book of Records* now. In 1990 *AIF* also received another accolade, the 'What The Papers Say' award in Britain as Newspaper of the Year. *AIF* has recently become a co-operatively owned weekly, independent of its previous publisher, the Knowledge Society. But, of course, we have always been editorially independent and this in the past has provoked much trouble for us.

The paper was started just over ten years ago with an initial circulation of 10,000 copies. Then it started doubling and trebling and eventually, soaring ahead of all others, to thirty-three million copies in 1990. Another remarkable figure – there are six People's Deputies now working on the paper, five elected to the Russian Parliament, the sixth a deputy to Moscow council. So our editorial board and the newspaper got the chance not just to speak of people's needs but to directly help them.

The paper is written by two dozen journalists, mostly young people under thirty. We get between five and seven thousand letters a day and they come from all over the country – both from godforsaken villages in Siberia, and buildings at the walls of the Kremlin. This is a real avalanche which covers our newspaper offices every day. It is also the powerful sound, the voice of a great people – where the voice of a child merges with that of a general or with that of a veteran who came through all the wars of the twentieth century. Sometimes it is like a fine tune, sometimes it more resembles a groan or a weep. These letters are as a result of the evolution of Soviet society. For decades this society used to live without legal freedoms and human rights. Its citizens were virtually deprived of all civil rights. This was a society which was badly informed. This was a society where a person could not freely live in or travel across his or her own country, to say nothing of travelling abroad. This was a society where citizens clashed with almost totally corrupted authority. And this society forced people with problems to seek a helping hand at our paper's editorial offices, which is often seen as the last resort. These people have come through all the bureaucratic channels and have been given all kinds of refusals, polite and impolite.

These letters show how unprotected individuals are against power in the USSR. They explain why Mikhail Gorbachev and Boris Yeltsin started on their monumental work – to release the Soviet people from the chains of totalitarianism. They show how hard the work is. Readers write about different problems, not just the political ones. But they also tell us, too, about the human soul. They show us how Russians act in their everyday life, how they bring up their children, what their major worries are – housing problems, lack of money, malnutrition, inadequate education, conscription and the army, and sometimes the KGB. These problems are projected on to every person's life. All of this is concentrated in these letters. There are ridiculous and naïve letters, there are letters in which people express their firm belief in a better future, or the will to change this world.

Listen to the voice of our people.

– Vladislav Starkov, Editor-in-Chief, *Argumenty i Fakty*
Moscow, November 1990

INTRODUCTION

The Soviet Union is composed of fifteen republics, almost 300 million people comprising more than 100 nationalities. It is the largest country in the world, where night never completely falls, and where crossing it by train takes more than a week (forget the roads!). It is a country of superlatives, many of them gruesome: the latest reliable estimates put the numbers of dead through the period of revolution – from the storming of the Winter Palace, then the Civil War, the Great Patriotic War and the blood madnesses of Stalin – at more than 100 million ('No one was keeping count,' Khrushchev). It is a country of enormous contrasts, from climatic to economic. It is, arguably, a country no more, as different republics – including the largest, the Russian Federation – serve notice of secession from Lenin's great creation, the Union of Soviet Socialist Republics.

In the seventy-plus years since the State's creation there have been two constants, the party and shortage, an odd cement for any society. Yet, until the first fissures began to open with Gorbachev in 1985 it held the union together, albeit often unwillingly. These two constants dominate this book.

The party and the State have been inseparable, controlling the civil service, the *nomenklatura*, the infrastructure, the military, the means of repression. Even today (at least at the time of writing) the party still controls the armed forces and the Internal Ministry and without the tacit support of the CPSU's (Communist Party of the Soviet Union) apparat the

USSR is ungovernable. Gorbachev's unparalleled task has been to strive to create a new, just society around and through the skeleton and nerve lines of the old – more political transubstantiation than perestroika.

Deprivation, shortage – from famine and starvation in the twenties and thirties, war, to the consumer blight of the last few years, and always, the absence of free speech – have accompanied the years of communism while successive governments have been careless at best, profligate at worst, of the country's enormous natural resources, consisting more than anything else of its people. The Soviet people have surely sacrificed more than any other in history for an ideal, however deformed at times it became in the hands of its protectors.

Expressions of dissent, of outrage, have been ruthlessly suppressed and the Press has traditionally been an arm of government and party. Lenin's dictum was that information was propaganda and that this propaganda should be at the service of the State. Only in August 1990 was censorship finally abolished and freedom of the Press enshrined in the constitution. Even today (autumn 1990) the party still owns and controls the major printing presses throughout the country and can turn them off to any dissident opinion. Shortage of newsprint (paper is allocated by the State) is another problem. The popular monthly *Novy Mir* produced only two issues in the first half of 1990 after announcing it was going to be producing the complete work of Solzhenitsyn and was deluged by a million extra subscribers.

Argumenty i Fakty (Arguments and Facts) was born into the 'period of stagnation', the Brezhnev years, in 1979. It was founded by Vladislav Starkov, an engineer turned journalist, who produced it – the first issue on his kitchen table – for the Znanie (Knowledge) Society, a sort of supercharged Workers' Educational Association which organizes lectures and funds publications. The introductory issue went to 10,000 subscribers and in the first year the newspaper received just thirty-five letters. In 1989, now with over thirty million subscribers, the paper received more than half a million letters. *Argumenty i Fakty* is the largest-selling and most widely read publication on the planet. Around 100 million Soviet adults, more than half of the adult population

– from Sakhalin Island through Siberia and Central Asia to the Kremlin – read the weekly. It is now bought by more than 34 million people and, because of newsprint shortages, recently appealed to any dissatisfied subscribers to reclaim their subscriptions so that frustrated potential buyers could be served.

Argumenty i Fakty has become the postbag of perestroika. Its importance is impossible to overstate, influencing government, producing legislation based on readers' suggestions. The paper is entirely reader-led. Apart from its letters columns, virtually all of the paper is fuelled by its public – interviews, for instance, are constructed round the most popular enquiries, 'Mikhail Sergeevich, thousands of our readers want to know why . . .'

Letters to the paper are really letters to Gorbachev, appeals for help, suggestions for changes in legislation, criticisms and rarely praise – but then people don't write to newspapers with congratulations. The paper's daily postbag is more than 7,000 letters and Starkov has survived a demand from Gorbachev for his resignation over his 'inflammatory' journalism. He and five other people on the paper were, early in 1990, elected People's Deputies, members of the Russian parliament (one to the Moscow Council). In March 1990 *AIF* was named Newspaper of the Year by Granada TV and the BBC's *What The Papers Say* programme.

This book is neither a history nor a sociology of the Soviet Union; there are many excellent ones available. It is a series of windows, illuminating observations and judgments on the state of the new society. Editorial comment has been kept to a minimum, intruding only to explain points, events or customs which may mean nothing in the West.

Boris Pasternak wrote, of the disastrous policy of forced collectivization – but his words are more widely applicable – that it was

> an erroneous and unsuccessful measure and it was impossible to admit the error. To conceal the failure people had to be cured, by means of terrorism, of the habit of thinking and judging for themselves, and forced to see what didn't exist, to assert the very opposite of what their eyes told them.

Here is the evidence the 'cure' failed. Editor Starkov says:

People abroad don't understand our culture shock. Not being free, not having to make decisions is easy. The shock is having to accept being individually and personally responsible for our lives. There is nothing more difficult to learn than what to do with freedom. How can you in the West, who have never not been free, understand this?

In early summer in Moscow the real price of a kilo of cherries (as opposed to the unavailable state price) was twelve roubles, more than a day's wage for a Russian. Put another way, it would cover the average cost of a month's rent and heating on a flat, if you were lucky enough to have one. A kilo of potatoes was available for a mere six hours' labour. Queues formed and snaked out of shops on the rumour, usually false, of goods arriving. In warm sunshine in the grounds of Kolomenskoye, an old Tsarist country estate beautifully situated on a long bend of Moscow River, I overheard one old babushka tell another, 'Do you hear, there's a shortage of coffins now.'

There's a grim humour, an indomitability about the Soviet people which is captivating, humbling. 'At least we aren't starving' you hear constantly. You remind yourself of that, faced with your hotel's unchanging menu, hard-boiled eggs or not. This is a country where Nescafé is a hard currency. This is the country which broke the Nazi army, the point of fracture marked, a few kilometres outside Moscow, by enormous, monumental St Andrews-crossed tank defences. The country which, while its men died in droves in its defence in their Great Patriotic War (the USSR's term for their involvement in the Second World War from 1941), took apart 1,523 crucial front-line factories, brick by brick, washer by washer, and transhipped them by train and reassembled them in the Urals and Kazakhstan to continue the war effort. And, in the Cold War peace, continued the war against its people ('It loves blood, the Russian earth.' Akhmatova).

Any understanding of the appetite for perestroika has to start with an appreciation of the sacrifices, the famines, the terror, the blood dues paid by the people. And of the paranoia of the leaders after Stalin, who had survived his whims, his purges, the destruction and rebuilding of the country. The mercurial Khrushchev probably best exemplifies this: the man who first denounced Stalin's opponents, and then later, famously, Stalin himself at the twentieth party congress (almost as Soviet tanks crushed the Hungarian revolution); the man who smashed his shoe on the table at the United Nations, and rolled nuclear weapons almost to the shores of the United States; who promised in 1961 that by the 1980s the Soviet Union would be outproducing the USA in industrial goods, and, arguably, was proved right – in the postwar period the economy grew faster than the American, industrial output more than twice as fast, agricultural output 80 per cent faster. But he was also the man who took away the right of peasants to have private plots and animals, cut away more than a quarter of the country's food supply and dislocated the young people from the land.

Gorbachev, whose speciality is agriculture, introduced co-operatives to the economy. And the free market in food, combined with chronic inefficiency in farming – up to one third of the Soviet harvest each year is lost – is responsible for the summer prices of cherries and potatoes in the private markets. Out of and around these co-operatives has grown a mafia, the gangster gangs responsible for widespread theft, extortion and corruption, which the militia (the police) seem unable or unwilling to combat. Influence and favour has always been an important economic lubricant in this society, 'Blat' as it's known, and there is an enormous Blat Pack.

President Gorbachev has pledged to make the rouble convertible and in July 1990, recognizing the large hordes of illegally held foreign currency, allowed these dollars and pounds to be declared and banked in special accounts without penalty, then had second thoughts. Not that the Russian rouble holder is poor: the amount of disposable income is high and statistically each Soviet man, woman and child holds a bank balance of more than 1,000 roubles (half a year's wages), albeit at a lowly interest rate of 2.5 per cent – while the admitted inflation is over 9 per cent (and most experts agree it is at more than 11 per cent).

For women abortion is used as the main method of birth control – there are more abortions than live births in the Soviet Union – and divorce is simple. But by the main indices of health, the Soviet citizen is less well, is indeed much less likely to survive birth, than his Western counterpart.

In old age, pensions are poor (this, at least, mirrors the

West) and the sector worst provided for is the former peasantry, collective farm workers. Veterans of the Great Patriotic War remain more privileged (or perhaps less underprivileged) than other pensioners. A bemedalled gerontocracy is evident on the streets, hoping for a route to the head of the queue, to extra coupons for scarce goods.

In a State hotel outside Moscow I mused over a dysfunction in the central planning system: there were no knives, but a glut of spoons. Somewhere in the Urals, I thought, there is a similar hotel where people are taking their soup off knives. And just then President Gorbachev was being asked in Parliament, 'what is going to become of us?' The man is not without humour. In reply he amended an old saying of the White Army, *'zgranitsa nam pamoshit'* (foreign countries will help us). Smiling, he said, 'Bush will help us.'

Well, perhaps. The following may be of some help too.

CHAPTER ONE

SOCIETY

HOUSING

Housing in the Soviet Union, while cheap, is poor and in desperately short supply. Young married couples traditionally stay for years with parents accumulating overcrowding points, and children. Families can be housed both by the State and through their work, in buildings owned by State enterprises. Private property is now legal and co-operatives have sprung up, rather like the old friendly societies, to build apartments and dachas for their members. It will cost as much for a Sony TV as a flat.

I was brought up in a children's home and never had a place of my own until I was forty-three. I raised two children; my son is an officer in the navy, his wife is a post-graduate medical student with a grant of R120 a month. They have a four-year-old daughter. These past four years, my son, when ashore, has been without a home. His wife has a tiny room in a student hostel, the little girl lives with her maternal grandparents. It's a great occasion for her when she sees both her parents together. She often asks her grandparents to tell her that she has a mummy and a daddy, like other children. There is no chance that they will get a flat.

My daughter is a programmer, she has a family and lives in a flat. What sort of government is it which allows only selected people to live normal family lives? Why is it that people in authority have everything, flats, dachas and money, and the others have nothing? I know what your answer will be – one has to work for it.

My son works hard, he is respected and praised in his work, and yet he has no place to live. He is at sea for 1–2 months at a time and when he comes ashore there is nowhere to go, so he stays on the ship. How long can this go on for? He is a high-class specialist, yet he lives like a tramp.

I have had a hard life, right from the cradle. Now my children are grown up, you would think I could relax a bit at last. But no, it's even harder in a way, when I think about my little granddaughter who is growing up without a home and without parents – even though they are both alive.

In Tsarist Russia, an engineer enjoyed a good life: he was esteemed and respected, he had money, he had a house and servants to look after him and his family. Today, an engineer has a degree and R120 a month. Nothing else, and this at the time when he is starting his own family. I would like to see Mikhail Gorbachev or other government officials trying to survive on those R120 a month. My life is already behind me. I have struggled on, always hoping for better, but it just gets worse and worse. How much longer do we have to suffer? When will an engineer regain his position, his authority? When will our young people live like human beings, with even the most basic necessities? If our government does not care about people, people will look for other ways and means to improve their situation; some will steal, others will leave the country.

I am a simple woman. I used to believe in our government. Now I believe no longer.

M. F., Kharkov.

(*Qualification for inclusion on the State housing list in the Soviet Union usually depends on an overcrowding factor. A square metre minimum per person – five or six metres – is the normal yardstick – Ed.*)

THE government has promised to provide each family with an apartment or house by the year 2000. Though the situation in the country is tense and it is extremely difficult to fulfil this promise I would like to ask again what the government means when it says 'every Soviet family'?

Our local authorities have established a limit of six square metres per person in State-owned blocks of flats. This could mean that at least seven people of two families have to share a standard forty-one-square-metre three-room apartment for one family to be entered on the waiting list. Does this mean that I, a thirty-two-year-old woman, my baby, my former husband and his parents have to live together to the end of our days? There is hardly anyone who would agree to exchange apartments with us, for we are on the ground floor, have a five-square-metre kitchen and damp communicating rooms, without a telephone or balcony. The authorities refuse to enter us on the list on some pretext or another. Is the problem considered solved if there is no one on the list?

L. Alyoshina, Makeyevka.

FIVE years ago I made up my mind to build a new house, a stone house, in place of the old one. Such a decision is not taken by many people. The estimated price I was quoted for this was R13,000. This year due to the increase in construction materials this price has gone up to R16,000. I don't have any savings and everything I spend goes on my house. Every year I have to pay 1 per cent tax on the cost of the house – R160. We pay house insurance which means we will be compensated if the house is destroyed for any reason. We pay land rent which is easily understandable as we took a piece of State land. But as to the tax on construction, this isn't clear. Don't taxes like this have an influence on those people who want to build their own house?

If I had known about the existence of such a tax before I started the construction – or, to be more precise, about the size of it – I would have thought twice. Wouldn't it be better to wait for five or seven years, save your money and mental health and get a State flat instead of all this for which you will pay much less than for your own house?

G. Alexeev, Alexin.

WHY is it that none of our People's Deputies have ever raised the issue of the lack of legal guarantees on private property? I mean a house. While I construct it and try to equip it, it is considered to be my property. I get no help from the State to do this. But if the city executive committee decides to build a bigger house on the site of my house they can and I have no say. They don't even need to consult with the house owner. He is given a State flat instead.

But as me and my wife are pensioners this flat will go back to the State when we die. But for my house, with three rooms, central heating, telephone, etc. they propose to pay to me R5,920. However, a similar flat sold by the State to citizens goes for four or five times as much. Why is there this difference? That's why I think it's necessary to have legal rights on private property when your home can be taken away like this. It would be more justifiable if I were given a similar flat to my own – from the point of area and equipment – in a municipal building. And of course I'm not even taking into account all the expenses incurred in the removal from my flat to a State one.

Y. Levin, pensioner, Kaluga.

THERE is a law that there should be living space per person of nine square metres. In some places even twelve square metres. It could be they are telling lies!

V. A., Tomsk.

IN our great country there are many families consisting of a mother and a daughter or a father and a son and the law is unjust to them. Because they are entitled to only a one-room apartment. One should think about two grown-ups sharing such a flat. It's nothing but a hostel with conveniences. I think that it's high time to reconsider the law. It should run as follows. Every grown-up person has the right to a separate room, irrespective of his or her sex. Children of nine or twelve should be considered to be adults.

Zamsha, Rostov on the Don.

THE rural citizens, the backbone of the country for 2,000 years, discover that the social and public consumption funds are not distributed in their favour. In civilized countries such funds are for the support of poor people. In our country they go to the most well-to-do. We pay the same as they do, those who live in State flats. But we built our own house with our own money. Through the public consumption fund we also help to pay for the dwellings of those who live in cities.

In cities, wages of workers are higher and for the millions of bureaucrats, higher still. We pay entirely for the water, gas and sewerage supplies to villages, we pay for the lighting and even for the red flags at celebrations. Our children are asked to stay in rural areas and even at school they try to impose on them some collective farm specialization. But we and our children practically don't use any free facilities, like sports complexes, art galleries and places of culture. As to vouchers, rural citizens use them less than other citizens because of a lack of means and time, as facilities and equipment and staffing in our hospitals, schools and kindergartens cannot be compared with those they have in cities.

And nowadays we are being surrounded, on all sides, by dachas. People who live in cities have a right to a second dwelling while those in rural areas do not have the right to get a flat in cities. With the construction of these dachas the shortage of construction materials became even more grave. People are constructing second dwellings and we cannot buy the materials for a first one!

The land given by local authorities to them is not at all worthless and when the dachniki settle they are not trying to hide how much they had to pay to buy this land. They are given meadowland and pastures and that's why there is no space left for our private cows. Even the collective farms' fields are being taken away.

And now the dachas are surrounded by fences and we are being separated from woods and rivers. The villages now look like concentration camps. To go to the wood now where our children used to play it's necessary to make a several kilometres, detour. And now there is nothing to pick in the woods, apart from bottles, cans and tanks and other waste. The roads and woods have been turned into rubbish tips. We are paying taxes on our land and dachniki use the land free of charge.

Watching TV we watch how citizens get irritated if any of their services are charged for, run on the self-accounting system. But there is nothing free of charge. For one person something may be free but this means that someone else is paying for it.

I want to draw your attention to the fact that most people who live in villages are old, who have worked on collective farms practically free of charge and now they receive extremely miserable pensions. How can they afford to pay R1,000–1,200 for the installation of gas, R400–600 for water supply and to pay all the taxes invented by the bureaucracy. All these taxes are paid in cash, and not only for them, but for the citizens whom they are supporting.

For example, if it's decided that the authorities need inventories of our property and animals, then we pay. Perhaps this office is now run on the self-accounting basis and this is how they get their wages and keep their jobs? Next, they'll probably decide that they need colour photos of our houses and dog kennels in 3-D. Or maybe they'll take pictures of villages from space to make us pay for a sputnik!

To transfer our houses to our children it's again necessary to pay 10 per cent of its cost though several generations may have invested time, materials and labour, including those who will inherit it. Children in villages, unlike city children, start to work and help early. Why should we pay the obligatory insurance? We want to remind you again that we have paid all this through the public consumption fund. This list could be continued. But it is high time we asked, where is justice? Taking into account that the majority of people in villages are old and they are less literate, less organized and they still have in them the fear of Stalinism – all this is used against them. They have virtually no access to the mass media information, they have no representatives in government or among the editorial people dealing with rural themes.

The authorities are afraid to make citizens of big cities pay for themselves. Tenants are more competent, more organized and the consequences of the self-accounting system imposed on them can be unpredictable. The government and other bodies are not interested in solving our problems. Because among the government and other supreme bodies there are people who are dachniki. That's why it's high time we had an open discussion of all these problems. It's high time debts are paid to the villages – not by idle promises about a bright future, but by roubles.

I would like sociologists and statisticians to work out all the figures on the above and our government and deputies give answers to the problems I've outlined.

A. Michahechev, deputy Rachmanovski rural council.

(Private individuals and enterprises pay into the public consumption fund which covers kindergartens, schools, hospitals, clinics, pioneer camps, etc. – Ed.)

I heard an official statement by the KGB on the radio today. It was about the victims of the Stalin-engineered purges. A total of approximately three million people were convicted and over 60,000 were sentenced to death by shooting.

There are people among us who are the innocent victims of this mindboggling arbitrariness. There may well be hundreds of thousands of them in this country.

They are the people who lost their families in those heinous purges and who for many years were deprived of their good name and could not live decent lives. At the end of their lives they still cannot afford a minimum of comfort to compensate for what they have gone through.

I have a friend who is about sixty years old now. In 1937, as a ten-year-old child, she lost her parents in the purges and had for ten years to live in orphanages in the Ryazan region and to take care of her younger sister.

People like this went through all possible hardships in their childhood and in their teens. Nothing changed as they grew older. They were treated as castaways. And yet they survived through the war, pulled through hunger and tuberculosis. What is most important is that they survived morally.

In 1947 the older sister (the one who is a friend of mine) left the orphanage and went to Moscow's Textiles Institute (she could not apply to any other institute with her record as a daughter of 'enemies of the people'). She lived on her tiny student grant for five years. Her diet was millet cooked with vegetable oil. She managed, however, to graduate with flying colours and was given a job placement in Moscow. She rented rooms for several years. Later she moved into a room in a flat that she started sharing with several more families [*multi-tenancy flats where the kitchen and other facilities are shared by several families; a result of the housing crisis in the Soviet Union*].

It so happened that this person, a woman of unusual character (which is only understandable) remained single. She worked in Moscow until she retired.

She still lives in her room in the four-room communal gulag that is destroying her nerves, and has no prospects of ever improving her housing situation.

There are tens of thousands of people like her in this country, including many single women, widows and children. No one cares for them. In order to qualify for a place on the State housing list they must be living in less than five square metres of floorspace.

Recently I spent some time looking through the telephone directory of the Supreme Soviet trying to identify who deals with this issue. I was told by somebody at the Committee for Social Policies that it did not come under their competence. The person I spoke to at the Committee for Legislation asked why I thought these people were worse off than others.

No doubt one can stock oneself with patience and spend a year or two making appointments with officials in various organizations in the hope that sooner or later one will come across a sympathetic official who, by way of a 'special case', will help the 'castaway' to get on to the State housing waiting list (where they will wait for another twenty years).

Is it not time for us to make such 'special cases' the rule by passing appropriate legislation?

N. Tairova, Moscow.

I am an engineer on a good salary. Over fifteen years ago I had a house built for my parents, who are retired collective farm workers, in a small village at the back of beyond. Every year I used to spend my holidays there (no chance of a holiday voucher for me!). Now my parents are dead. I had the house valued for insurance purposes by State Insurance (R16,000), but was told by them that I could not insure the house as the legal owners were my parents. Tell me, how could any retired collective farm worker, whose pension was in the range of R12–40 per month, have built a R16,000 house and paid high State Insurance annual premiums on top of that?

Now I am told that I must buy my own house again. I have to fill in an 'inheritance form' (half a page of printed matter, fee: R1,600). The market price of a house in such a remote locality is approximately R2,000 and I do not want to sell it, anyway. Inheritance should be one's right, not a duty, but of course, officials know best how to squeeze blood out of a stone. Some time in September 1989 I read a reply to a similar question in *AIF*. The reply was written by the USSR Ministry of Finance. They said that next of kin legatees would soon be exempt from this disgraceful tax. No such luck for me. I have proof that the house was built with my money and that I personally helped with the building work. No one is interested, they won't even listen to me. I'd like to ask a question: is there another country where decent, law-abiding citizens are treated with the same callousness and indifference? If I were an alcoholic, for example, I would be given lots of attention: free treatment, medication etc. As I am a decent citizen who uncomplainingly helps to maintain hordes of non-productive bureaucrats, I get nothing but trouble.

P. Berestne, Kuibyshev.

THESE days, many Russian families would gladly forsake 'the sunny republics' of Central Asia and return to their native Russian land. Not so easy, though.

These are turbulent times for the southern districts; few are willing to exchange their flats in order to live in an 'exotic' place. And to give up one's hard-won flat simply seems impossible.

Surely there must be a simple way out?

How about saying that a person wanting to move should hand over his or her flat to the local housing authorities, for example somewhere in Uzbekistan, and then move, with the family, to a town in Russia. There, local housing authorities provide the family with a flat, similar to the one they have left behind. Both localities belong to the same State. There is one central housing fund for the whole country. The State won't lose a single square metre of housing space in such an exchange.

But then again, I wonder? Handing over one's flat is easy, no problem. But to get one in exchange – that's different. Chance would be a fine thing. It is time to do something about this.

B. Kalinin, Angren, Tashkent province.

ADDRESSING the Congress of People's Deputies, A. Yemelianov spoke about overcrowded flats shared by several families and comfortable houses for the élite.

We are builders about to build one such house at 20/22 Sivtsev Vrazhek, Moscow. Commissioned by the administration of the Communist party's Central Committee, the specification calls for state-of-the-art design, improved interior layout and the highest quality materials. Three apartment buildings were pulled down to make room for this house and the former tenants given flats on the outskirts of Moscow. The building has a day-care facility for élite children.

Why, in spite of glasnost and the decisions of the Congress, do party officials get everything immediately while ordinary people still have to wait for years to get a new flat, happily agreeing to go to the remotest suburbs?

Though the country is reviving Lenin's principles of justice, this leftover of the stagnation period continues to flourish.

The *Good Evening Moscow* programme, a live Moscow TV show, asked the chairman of the Kiev district party committee about the fate of this house but he didn't get a clear answer. We urge the administration department of the party's Central Committee to give this house to large families with lots of children.

As for the 'people's servants', party officials, they should be put on the waiting list and get new housing in line with the recommendations of the Congress to eliminate all benefits for party officials.

Building workers, Construction Board 201: fifty-one signatures.

(*As a result of this letter the house was relinquished by the party for occupation by 'non-élite' families – Ed.*)

PENSIONS

IT'S pleasing to realize how much our State cares about pensioners. But the district committees on social insurance require documentary confirmation of one's working years before old people can qualify for a proper pension. Many of us are over seventy and to increase the miserable allowance even up to R70 a month requires this written evidence.

But it often happens that many are from State collective farms or from different agricultural projects which no one even remembers. Nevertheless, it's necessary for the social insurance authorities to have a reference that the archives of the enterprise or collective farm where a pensioner worked have not been preserved. Additionally it's necessary to find not less than two witnesses who have known the person in their joint work on the collective farm.

During the forced collectivization of farms and the destruction of the peasantry [*in the twenties and thirties under Stalin*] hundreds of thousands of villages in our country simply disappeared and there are not archives on all of them. From where is it possible to find witnesses?

It may be all right if a pensioner has relatives to look after such things but if a person is single or ill, then what happens? The point is not just this. Even if old people can get all of this information for the social insurance committees they are humiliated, driven to tears. One babushka, my neighbour, told me 'I worked for twenty years on a collective farm and no one even thanked me for it. Where can I now find the office of this collective farm because on the place where it had been, long ago, only grass grows.'

I am writing this letter on behalf of my mother who during the war we practically didn't see because she was always at her work. For her 'striking labour' she got governmental commendation signed by Stalin and Gorky where it is written 'the Motherland never forgets your labour'. Why is it necessary to invent problems for these old people? There are only a few of them left.

A. Necrilova, Omsk.

(*Those who worked on State farms have the lowest pensions in the Soviet Union – Ed.*)

IN honour of forty years of victory it was decided to give 20 per cent pension increases to the participants of the Great Patriotic War. However, there was one stipulation. That this addition is only valid for those who have worked without interruption at the same enterprise for not less than twenty-five years. I have a total working period of more than thirty-five years, not at the same enterprise but at two. Both are Soviet State enterprises and my transfer from one to the other was ordained for some 'objective reason'.

The pension decree was published with the aim of further improvement of the welfare of the participants of the Great Patriotic War and as a modest tribute from the State for their contribution to the victory. It is linked, nevertheless, to the total working period at the same enterprise and it turns out that not all of the participants of the war have the same rights. Not all of them can get the same care and attention from society, but only selectively. Of what social justice can we speak in this case? It is a mere symbolic gesture.

V. Makharov, Bersk.

I read in *AIF* an article about the designing of monuments dedicated to the victims of repression from the thirties through to the fifties. Here is my proposal, helping the victims not by stones but by a real deed. Most of the victims are still alive.

In 1950 I was sent to a concentration camp in the north of our country for ten years, from the fourth course of the Odessa Institute of Engineers of the Marine Fleet. The reason was, I heard a joke in which our leader was mentioned. I didn't go to the KGB to tell on those who were present and who told the joke. That was my crime. I was twice given the opportunity to inform but as I categorically refused I spent all these years in the camp until 'the father of all peoples' died. To be exact, I spent another year and a half there – until 1954.

And what do I need, personally, as a former victim of Stalin's repressions? Only one thing. To include in my work-ing years' period my stay in the concentration camp where I worked twelve hours a day, every day of the year. I managed to survive until pension age. On the certificate given to me on liberation it is written 'pardoned by the Praesidium of the Supreme Soviet of the USSR'. My 'conviction' was purged.

Our district executive does not include my years of forced labour in my qualification for pension and won't until I bring along another certificate of 'rehabilitation'. I wrote a letter to the Praesidium in August 1988 and my letter was given to the general prosecutor who sent it to Kiev: from Kiev it was sent to Sinfiropa and from there to Sebastopol where I live. Then the letter was sent to Odessa where I was 'judged'. They sent it to Kiev, from Kiev to Moscow and it has taken more than a year for application for rehabilitation to circulate and still nothing is solved.

E. Balavin, member of the CPSU, veteran of labour, inventor,
Sebastopol.

I am an old age pensioner, or to be more exact, a former pensioner. Because, in 1987 I went to live in Italy. In exchange for the passport they told me to hand in my work book and my pension certificate. In this way I was deprived of my right to a pension which I had been working for all my life.

Let me give you the explanation. In 1980 my daughter married an Italian and went to live in Italy. I visited them several times. Now I'm alone because my husband died and they invited me to live in Italy with them. I thought about it and agreed. But now I'm deprived of the pension only because I went to live with my daughter. At the social security department I was told that my children could support me.

Here in Italy they pay a social pension even to women who never worked in their lives but I'm not entitled to it because I remain a citizen of the Soviet Union. That's why the Soviet government and not the Italian government must take care of my old age. And that's why I suggest that the new law on pensions should have a provision that all of the citizens who have left the Soviet Union have a right to get their pensions.

Bolshikova, Italy.

(The Supreme Soviet passed sixty new laws in the twelve months to June 1990 with a further 108 in draft. On the proposed pensions law they received more than 500,000 letters – Ed.)

WHY don't we appreciate the efforts put by women into raising their children? A woman is supposed to have a choice: whether she wants to enter employment or focus on her children. Many mothers who have several children have to work to earn their pensions. As a result their children are not properly looked after which sends juvenile crime spiralling.

I suggest that women be entitled to old age pensions upon reaching retirement age no matter the length of their work record. These pensions need only be the bare minimum.

N. Novikova, Leningrad.

PRIVILEGE

FROM the deep recesses of human history the unwritten laws for living together have been handed down to us, from times when it was just not right to have parties, weddings or large gatherings at times when everyone was helping to bring in the harvest, laying down stores of food and preparing for the harsh winter.

During the summer everyone worked their fingers to the bone to get the food in. Nowadays we seem to have chosen to ignore these sacred rules.

Without the slightest hint of shame, people go visiting friends, no doubt thinking that they are doing something really worthwhile for society. At the height of the harvesting and processing season a six-hundred-strong delegation headed by the top bosses left the Ukraine to go off and strengthen our friendshp with Kazakhstan, where they no doubt prevented a further 600 people from attending to their own vital business there.

Can they really not do this in November and December?

Doubtless each and every participant in this event considers that by his very presence he is inspiring all of us 'to labour and victories' in the name of the common good. Not on your life! In fact they are doing the very opposite.

Now is not the time for 'inspiration' to come to us through a famous Ukrainian actress posing for the TV cameras in front of a field of ripe melons somewhere in Central Asia, while back at home in Kiev (and no doubt in other cities as well), there's not a single tomato in the shops despite the season being at its height. They tell us that there just aren't enough people to pick them. So whose job is it to organize enough pickers?

Perhaps if we sang, danced and made merry less, we would get further.

M. Smokov, manual worker, Kiev.

I saw a television report recently of the arrival in Moscow of a large group of Second World War veterans, who were coming to take part in a parade on Red Square. As I watched it I thought of how the fortieth anniversary of Victory was celebrated in the town where I live.

The combined column of war veterans, among whom was my father aged seventy-five, bearing his many medals, was marching past the tribune where members and associate members of the district party committee stood, people who had never so much as sniffed gunpowder in their entire lives. And when my elderly father reached the tribune, and wanted to stop for a few seconds to catch his breath, he was chivvied on by the various militia men on duty there. After the parade as he told me about this there were tears in his eyes. He also told me another story.

One of the men he served with, who was also the holder of many Soviet medals, had worked for many years as a metal worker, and was put in charge of servicing the air conditioning and central heating system in the tribune. Can you just imagine the scene? Holiday atmosphere, the tribune with its load of civic notables, including the first secretary of the Komsomol district committee, who was a young lad who had not long ago graduated and was listlessly waving to the people as they filed past – and underneath, in the semi-darkness, a grey-haired war veteran in his holiday best, with all his medals and orders on his chest, keeping an eye on the temperature gauge.

Is it not now time in our democratic society to change this outdated tribune system left over from the times of stagnation? Why is it that every town and city still has its tribunes where only members of the district or city party committee are entitled to stand, while all other party workers have to stand next to the tribune with their wives and children? I don't suppose that all of them have taken their turn at filing past in the parades either. When they were children they used to stand with their parents near the tribune while their school-friends marched past, and when they grew up and inherited their 'rightful' posts, they began to put their own children at the foot of the tribune. Just look and see how many children and grandchildren of the highly placed there are on the guest tribune in Red Square during parades, yet to them this is all perfectly natural, that is where they always are.

It seems to me that everyone, regardless of the position they hold, should be obliged to take part in these parades and to file past, to symbolize the unity of workers throughout our State. And if somebody has got to wave to them from the tribune, then it should only be people who by their work or feats of arms have really deserved that right.

A. Dukhov, Semipalatinsk.

HOW much does a gloss veneer cost? During my life I have had many opportunities to take part in and observe VIP meetings. Immediately after the Second World War I found myself picking up cigarette ends, counting blades of grass, sweeping up, repainting and perking up various military towns with my troops. After 1950, when I was no longer in the army, I was involved in preparations for visits by ministers, district committee secretaries, the Ukrainian Central Committee and the USSR Central Committee. I was lucky enough to get a close-up view of Shelest, Shcherbitsky, Khrushchev, Brezhnev, even the four-engine train that used to bring Stalin back from the south.

I wonder exactly how much money was spent on these clean-up operations, and how many people were taken away from their main jobs in order to do them?

The last such visit I witnessed was Ligachev's visit to agricultural workers in the city of Kharkov.

What deception there was! The delegates were going to visit food and vegetable stores and the market in the huge new borough of Salmovka, which houses 300,000 people. Plane loads of fresh cucumbers, tomatoes and greens from private hothouses were flown in; tinned food, fresh meat, sausage, different sorts of fish. They provided the market with new stalls built by master craftsmen. Then they drafted in dozens of militia and officers of the law in uniform and plain clothes. God preserve us from anyone happening to glance in at the window and see all this spit and polish and piles of fresh produce.

It only took half an hour to get all the ceremonials over and done with, for the visitors to leave, and then the stores were closed and stripped bare of everything that had been brought in from the private hothouses and stores. Fifteen to twenty minutes later the shelves were as bare as they had ever been.

Then that evening in his televised speech Mr Ligachev spoke eloquently about the wonderful array of foodstuffs on sale in Kharkov, and the cameras showed the market stalls from which the government hadn't sold a single rouble's worth of food.

I quite often nowadays watch televised coverage of our leaders' journeys about the country. Every time I see one of them I see a re-enactment of Kharkov.

I haven't ever seen any of them stopping off at a run-down village at the door of a poor old woman whose barn roof is caving in and whose cottage is falling down around her ears. I have never seen them visiting shops with absolutely nothing to put on their shelves.

I am haunted by a single thought.

Do our leaders really not know or understand that this waste of money, this glossing over these elaborate security measures all boomerang back on them and reduce their credibility in the eyes of honest people everywhere?

They say that after the war Kalinin used to walk around Moscow without a bodyguard, and that during Stalin's times when Postyshev [*a highly placed government official*] was queuing for food the shop girl emptied the food he had bought into his hat.

Nowadays you wouldn't see any of them on the streets. Even the least significant of them manages to drive around in a black Volga, and the next level above in a black Volga with his own personal guard. To guard him from whom one wonders?

A. Pelikh, Kharkov.

I am a pensioner. For more than twenty years I worked on the staff of the regional trade department. And I know that on the staff of ministries of trade and regional trade departments there are people whose job it is to measure consumer demand for goods. Keeping in mind the present situation, it's hardly necessary to investigate the demands of buyers. I propose these people be made redundant, at least until there are goods in the shops, and the money used to keep strict control of the division of goods to people.

A pensioner, Kiev region.

CEREMONY

THE *Vremya* [Time, *a national news television prime time programme*] said yesterday that the government had decided to stage a military parade on Victory Day. In my view no military parade should be held this year (1989) because it is a difficult and unpopular year both at home and internationally. If we do we would be holding ourselves up to ridicule. The economy is in pieces. The Soviet Army has been declared an army of occupation by several European countries and Soviet Republics. Monuments to Soviet soldiers are being desecrated. Members of the armed forces are being shot down in Azerbaijan and Armenia because their commanders have failed to authorize them to defend themselves, servicemen's families have been driven away, and the army has been degraded. The list goes on. Can there be any question of staging a Victory Day parade in such a situation?

I believe that the funds that have been allocated for this feast of self-eulogizing and prestige-boosting enjoyed by the party and the top military should be spent on helping the families of servicemen who have been left in desperate conditions or have been wounded in Azerbaijan, Armenia, Central Asia, Afghanistan, Eastern Europe or the Baltics. To hold a parade now would be a mockery of people and their problems.

E. Kontsov, war veteran.

THE WAR

THROUGH your newspaper I would like to express thanks – I'm not quite sure to whom – for the privileges recently bestowed on us veterans of the Great Patriotic War. In October we were all given special green books in which we could order cars, refrigerators, furniture, washing machines and other goods. When I counted the time that I would have to wait for such things I was amazed at how long we were all expected to live! Because if we order any of these things the shortest time we would receive any of them would be ten years. We will be getting a car in 100 years, a refrigerator in fifty years – and so on.

To tell the truth, when the majority of us are over seventy, we don't need such things ourselves. We could only speculate with them or give them to relatives. Nobody seems to have thought of this. Now, we can't even buy such things as inexpensive coats, suits, linen or socks – they aren't available no matter what colour of book. Maybe it is that those who gave us these 'privileges' want us to walk around in our birthday suits? Everything seems to point that way. Are us veterans of the war worthy of such humiliation? Perhaps someone can tell me.

D. Ventskeyvich, Moscow.

ALL of the participants of the Great Patriotic War have medals with Stalin's profile. As we know now, this man betrayed socialism and it was his fault that millions of people perished. I propose to collect all the medals with his image which exist in our country and to melt them and recast them. The new medal will be a big one, and beautiful, with the inscription, 'for the merits in victory, 1941–1945'. I think that all veterans will be proud to carry it.

N. Sasnovsky, veteran of labour, Ulanady.

WE have to stop dividing the participants in the Great Patriotic War into different categories. There should be one law which does not discriminate between them. Despite the fact that we were lying under the same blankets, ate the same bread and took the same dusty water, today, nevertheless, some are looking at others with envy. All this is a result of different benefits and privileges given to different categories of them.

One category, for example, receives six kilos of meat and sausages in cans, another only two kilos of meat and sausages, without cans. Do you think this is a minor thing? No. It is vicious when by consumer goods and foodstuffs your merits are judged by your Motherland and the people. Bullets did not discriminate. It was only by chance I was wounded. Benefits should be the same throughout the country to all who fought.

G. Shaen, settlement Sarata, Odessa region.

WE used to call the working class by many different descriptions: the leading class; excellent; the decisive force of perestroika. So how has it turned out that since 1922 this highly respected class has always had the shortest holidays. Now it's very much in fashion to talk about social justice but why is it that no one listens to a fitter or a lathe operator who has had to work for almost forty years to get at last an increase in holidays up to eighteen days. But all of the rest of the people have twenty-four.

Sociologists and economists say that the working class is declining in number. Is that so surprising because who is going to choose a way of life that is much worse in comparison with others?

L. Shin, worker, Kazan.

THE mass heroism and the deeds of our soldiers during the war with fascism are well known. But up to now for the majority of our people, heroic deeds by the army of our enemy have been like a State secret. Whether they had their own Alexander Matrosovs and General Karbusheveys and whether the German soldiers undertook such heroic actions as we did hasn't been known. For example, all of us know very well that the best Soviet pilots Kushado and Pakrishkin destroyed in air battles sixty-two and fifty-nine enemy planes respectively. We had other top-class pilots. But the *Luftwaffe* had its heroes too. For example Erich Hartmann shot down 352 aircraft, Gerd Barrhorn 301 planes, Erich Rugdorfer 222. One hundred and four pilots of the *Luftwaffe* destroyed more than 100 aircraft each. Of 45,000 Soviet planes lost in air battles, 24,000 were destroyed by 300 German pilots.

I think that knowing the truth about this does not underestimate the deeds of our soldiers. But in fact it helps us understand what kind of war it was and to appreciate that we won the war sometimes not just by ability but by number, as for each German soldier killed in this war, for each destroyed tank or plane, sometimes we had to lose several of our soldiers, our tanks and planes. Our soldiers were not worse than German soldiers, our tanks and planes were not worse either. The leaders of the country were to blame, they were responsible. We who were waging the war were not taking into account losses and they were responsible for ruining the lives of millions.

U. Selivanov, serviceman.

BY Decree of the Praesidium of the USSR Supreme Soviet, those awarded the 'Victory Over Germany' Order are entitled to the title of 'Ex-Serviceman of the 1941–1945 War'.

In the past, all holders of the Order were given Victory Medals on subsequent anniversary occasions, i.e. twentieth, thirtieth and fortieth anniversary. Both medals and certificates were issued to 'Ex-Servicemen'.

However, when in the late 1970s the question of benefits arose, the authorities decided to withdraw the title of 'Ex-Serviceman' from all except Field Forces of the Red Army. Certificates were then issued only to those particular units. Red Army soldiers and officers who, in 1945, had been awarded the Victory Over Germany Order but had not been in the Field Forces during the war, were no longer given their certificates and lost their 'Ex-Serviceman' title.

Now, on Victory Days, our employers do not include us in the celebrations as ex-servicemen. We are not included with the rear services, either, as they are holders of a different order – 'Distinguished Labour in Wartime'.

Who are we?

27

It is not that we begrudge the Field Forces their benefits. Let them enjoy them, there is enough poverty in the country as it is. We are hurt because we have been ignored and stripped of our dignity as Red Army soldiers and officers who, though not on the battlefield, had made their contribution to the victory over the Nazis.

Yours respectfully,
ex-soldiers of the Red Army, Avertsev, Turov, Chepurin,
Popov, Baranov, Tesler, Lekhanov, Rykov, Pecherkin.
Perm.

SHORTAGES

IN our town we buy shoes by coupons. We are entitled to one pair of shoes a year. But what kind of shoes should one buy? One needs shoes for summer wear, for winter wear, to say nothing of spring or autumn. Maybe now they produce all-weather shoes and we don't know about it yet? Well, I'll keep my coupon for the time being to see if it is true.

Laguta, Svetlogorsk.

ON the eve of a holiday in the town of Privolzhsk, Ivanovo region, an enraged crowd forced its way into a milk store and down the stairs into its basement where wine is sold and crushed a 53-year-old man to death. Disgraceful practices in selling alcoholic drinks continue. Long lines, fights, extortion, bad language – all this takes place a hundred metres from the luxurious building of the district party committee and the district executive committee where bureaucrats, having tremendous powers, do not want to do anything to put the trade system in order.

A. Pesorin, Privolzhsk, Ivanovo region.

IN the Kremensk district, Luga region, cotton stockings are sold only for the deceased, on presentation of death certificates by relatives, and socks only to war invalids and Afghan war veterans. And what should we, the living, wear? Imported elastic stockings are not for village life and, incidentally, not everyone can afford them.

P. Slepets, Mstki village, Luga region.

WHEN the railway company sells you a ticket it is making you pay in advance for its services. The price of the ticket may vary considerably depending upon the volume and quality of the services offered.

I have travelled the length and breadth of the country and cannot remember a single occasion upon which the railway company has fulfilled all the conditions of the agreement I have had with them, or returned any money in compensation.

I'd like to take the rail service that I know best as an example.

The route between Moscow and Kishinev is usually express service only, some of the trains are foreign. For these express services we pay extra; however for a good while now they have been considerably non-express. For several years every single train on that line has unfailingly been late.

The ladies in the station information booths don't particularly want to have to talk to tired and irritable passengers, so they have put up boards saying 'Express [!] train No. 47 Moscow–Kishinev is running – hrs – mins late'. All they have to do is to chalk in the figures and they have saved themselves the trouble of repeating it a hundred times. They have made little boards like this for other services, Sofia–Moscow and back, Bucharest–Moscow and back.

Taking money for services not provided is robbery or extortion, call it what you will, and these are criminal offences. Not to mention the rest of the services which passengers in the different class carriages have paid for and which they likewise do not get. The railways ought at least to return them the premium they have paid for these.

I have another idea. Since the trains are regularly late, we should make it official; alter the timetable and call the services by a different name. The ticket price would have to reflect this.

L. Kazakov, journalist, Tiraspol, Moldavia.

CHARITY

Do we have a lot of charitable establishments? It could be that we could have dozens of canteens which function free of charge for poor people. According to data collected by the Empress Maria, in 1899 there were 14,857 such establishments with an income of R405 million. That's not taking into account private charity activities which were also rather widely developed. Hostels and alms houses were supported by private individuals.

Nowadays we have hundreds of thousands of people who are below the poverty line. The economic state of the country doesn't enable us to increase the level of social protection of such people. There is a shortage of means for the construction of hostels but at the same time in the suburbs of Moscow station Kakoshkina there is an asylum for old horses and in the park Lassini Ostrov there is a home being built for cats and dogs with a lot of room. However, the law does not permit private charity establishments for people.

I think it's necessary to do away with prohibitions on private charity activities, thus enabling people and organizations to open asylums and hostels for the homeless and free canteens. We need to make local councils provide premises for this purpose and render assistance in the purchase of the necessary tools and equipment.

Y. Tretchikov, Moscow.

This country has a lot of children and old people who have no relatives and have to be supported by the government's social schemes. Orphanages and homes for the elderly are normally situated far away from one another. Why not build them as complexes? Children would then be able to take care of elderly people, and the other way round. Children will have grandparents, as it were, and the elderly will have grandchildren.

They need one another. Learning to take care of elderly people will make children more caring citizens when they grow up. We should not worry that children will disturb the old people's peace. On the contrary, they will make their lives more enjoyable and, probably, longer.

They will know that there is somebody who cares and who needs them.

E. Kryuchkova, Moscow.

SEX & MORALITY

A friend of mine and I went to see an exhibition of erotic photography in our town, Kherson. What a revolting spectacle! Bodies everywhere, like hunks of meat. Everything exposed: breasts, bottoms, pubic hair. And faces ... either vacant or lewd. What has happened to beauty? We recognized some of the beauties from the photo-contest – also some of our local prostitutes. For example, Miss Photo '89!

The only thing that was missing was a photo-brothel, two roubles a piece. I read in the papers that the photo-exhibition was a purely commercial venture. Yes, I can see, 'through sexual stimulation to the wallet'.

I have seen a reproduction of Venus de Milo. Here you have a miracle, a pure vision of beauty, a vision sublime, which fills your soul with delight and admiration for the spiritual beauty of the maiden. I looked at our 'Venuses', pitiful, sordid, their maidenhood long forgotten ... men, who went to see the exhibition, left with a feeling that they'd visited a brothel. Well, every man to his taste. For me, it was two roubles down the drain. Young people should oppose the commercialism which seeps into all spheres of life.

Today, in our country, even souls are for sale, let alone bodies. And why were there no photographs of nude men at the exhibition? Clearly, models were not to be found. It's not fair. There should be a photo-contest for Superman '89. Imagine, what a delightful spectacle this would be . . .!

The saddest thing, though, is that there is no soul in those nude bodies, so gladly exposing themselves to the public eye. This is the whole tragedy.

D. Kireev, student, age 20.

IN recent times many of the age-old moral standards have started to be cast aside by certain officials responsible for the promotion of cultural activities and by the mass media who have described such standards as 'pre-perestroika prejudices'.

When they introduced the borrowed word 'sex' into our everyday vocabulary, these officials and editorial boards of newspapers and magazines found it possible to unveil, as it were, a sphere of human activities that had been taboo since time immemorial.

Again since time immemorial it has been improper to show children or even adults the 'culmination' of a couple's intimate relationship. If a society is not to become a herd of cattle it must protect this supreme even though unwritten law.

Who if not the older generations, parents who from their own and from their children's experience know in what way low morals can affect couples, who if not people who started families only to break up leaving their children unhappy and unsettled, should guard the moral standards, ethical laws and rules of conduct?

It is time that officials and the Press came to grips with the idea that only members of the older generations who have had a lot of experience, and not inexperienced young people, let alone 'immoral ladies' and those characters who use their services, should have the right to interpret and assert ethical laws and moral standards!

We stand for sexual education for young people aimed at consolidating the family and harmonizing people's sexual relationships.

Naturally, there is more to morals than just the ethics of sexual relationship but when such ethics come tumbling down the following categories follow suit: decency, honesty, humaneness, ability to feel for others and proper attitudes in all areas that are vital for the present generations and generations to come.

This makes us believe that modern society equipped as it is with the powerful mass media should pass laws to ban the use of any such media (video bars and cinema houses included) for the proliferation of base morals.

> This statement adopted by a session of the war and labour veterans, members of the Communist party, in the city of Krasnoyarsk.
> President of the meeting, *signed* (V. Peskowsky).
> Clerk of the meeting, *signed* (V. Sidorova).

IN October 1917 we thought we were the wisest people on earth. A great number of staunch Marxists, zealots of class morality, still think so. This wisdom is supposed to be apparent in all spheres of life in our socialist paradise. Particularly in regard to prostitution.

Since throughout the whole of its history mankind has not succeeded in getting rid of this supposed anachronism, there is very little chance that we shall be successful now. The worse a society stinks, the more the oldest profession flourishes.

There is a way out: to legalize it. As it is, we are the laughing stock of the world. A human being's physiological needs will only stop with his or her death. Their character can be changed and become more cultured or enlightened and this can be achieved through the soul and the spirit. It would not be easy. But we would not be the first to attempt it.

I am not for the legalization of prostitution because of any perverse cravings. I have a happy marriage and my wife and I will soon be celebrating our silver wedding anniversary. I see a prostitute first of all as a person who has her own views upon the matter and leads her life accordingly. Banning prostitution will not stop it from existing. Nor will Marxist dogmas.

Shouldn't we, at last, grow wiser?

V. Manzhos, Mamontovo, Altai.

I'M working as an instructor at the personnel department at a consumers' co-operative. Eighty per cent of the working people are women. They are young and beautiful and it's painful to see that they work in cold shops; in the winter they wear padded jackets and gloves when they stand behind the counter; they have to light fires in the stoves; they have to load and unload goods because in the seventy years of Soviet power practically nothing has been done to improve the working conditions of sales people in the rural areas. There has been no technological progress, no new shops, no houses, no roads have been built. And there is only one answer, no money, no money, no money.

Now they arrange beauty competitions – the main idea of

which is to glorify femininity. Dear women, we used to think that the woman has already glorified herself but it appears that if she doesn't display herself naked on the stage or the TV screen she will not glorify her femininity. They measure the length of legs, the breadth of hips, waist, shoulders and after examining her in a sitting, lying and standing position they award her the title of Miss USSR, because she is the most beautiful woman in the Soviet Union.

None the less, in my opinion it is a shame to award such a title to a girl because I cannot agree that she is the most beautiful girl among the rest of the girls in the USSR. She might be the most beautiful girl among the competitors, though. Very few girls take part in the competition, those who don't have to work. And they are certainly not peasant girls and working girls.

They have spent lots of money to arrange such competitions and then our beauties make a world tour; they are presented with cars, furs, royal attire and all this for the mere fact that their hips, their waist and their shoulders are better than the rest.

I believe that there are no ugly women but that there are circumstances that make a woman ugly. The money spent on the arrangement of beauty competitions should be spent on improving the working conditions of our women. I want these competitions to be stopped and I believe my demand will be supported by millions of other women in our country.

Kasatkila, village of Karsovi.

I'VE long been thinking about writing to the Ministry of Culture, but kept on putting it off in the hope that our new Members of Parliament would deal with the problem for us. A lot has been said about the educational role of the cinema, popular songs, rock music, etc. etc., but the people in charge of culture seem to have very little idea about what the state of our people's culture is, and even less idea about the economics of it, about how much the State loses when the people have no real culture. You don't have to be a doctor of economics to understand this. Over the last few decades people's treatment of each other has degenerated. Almost every day we see people being degraded, boorish behaviour and foul language from adults, teenagers and students alike; they no longer have any respect for their elders. And what do we see on our television screens? Half-naked savages and their soul-rending howling, almost every film shows the sexual act in great detail etc. etc. There are lots of small-time films full of murder and violence. What on earth are we teaching the rising generation? Film-makers try to tell us that their films are saying something. You switch on the radio and hear yet another pop group wailing like cats on a hot tin roof and wonder whatever prompted the programme planners to give them air time. I suppose the answer is that everyone is too busy thinking of filling their own pockets first. On behalf of hundreds, nay thousands of people, I demand that we should not be subjected to unpleasantness, vulgarity and dirt on our television screens.

Mr Kartushev, Chelyabinsk.

BUREAUCRACY

AUTHORITIES of our city are ready to spend several hundred thousand roubles on the planning of the central square of the city and on a statue of Lenin to be erected there. By the way, we already have three monuments to Lenin in our city.

An all-Russian competition was launched for the best design. They say (I don't know if it's true) that the bronze statue has already been brought to our city. But at the same time we have many problems. Our city clinic which is 100 steps from the central square looks run-down and everyone who passes can't help but notice it. We need to build more housing, a nursery, roads, a swimming pool, but there is no money. And I think a new central square could wait, given that the present one is quite decent and is even pictured in several postcards.

But nobody consulted the citizens on all this. The talks about this square happened only at a session of the State council in 1987. Estimates on how much it will all cost aren't known to us and we have hardly any information. Sometimes we just want to build things for the admiration of our foreign neighbours, from Finland and Sweden, who very often come to our city. But it seems that we don't think very much about our own citizens.

O. Bundur, Kandalaksha, Murmansk region.

ANNUALLY on the eve of 1 May and 7 November [*revolutionary holidays*] in our institute (as in many other institutes and organizations) an order is issued in accordance with which all working premises and laboratories should be inspected by a specially appointed commissioner and should be closed and stamped two or three hours before the end of the working day. [*Children make paper ribbons, threads and ties which are fixed across the doors and the seals stamped against unauthorized entry.*]

Due to all this the working day turns out to be a free day. What is the sense in all this if during the summer vacation periods some of the laboratories are closed sometimes for a month or more without this procedure at all?

Perhaps there is an instruction which was adopted long ago when it was thought that our class enemies never slept! So if anything untoward happened to these seals on those two days of the year our leaders would see it as a possible political action.

A.B., Moscow.

A new hotel has been built on Vertivosky Embankment in Gorky in the shortest time imaginable. It's a seven-storeyed palace with a luxurious entrance hall, columns, stairs covered with carpets and comfortable rooms with telephones and television sets. There is no sign on the hotel but when tourists leave the ships and walk along the embankment they admire the beauty of the magnificent palace and ask what kind of building it is. They are told that it's a hotel belonging to the regional party committee.

This palace has been built near a very old hospital for children. The buildings are one-storeyed and wooden, without any conveniences and with outdated medical equipment. The food is very bad. In this district in which 300,000 people live there is no bath house. Well, to be more exact there is one but it's in a very poor state. Five hundred metres away from the hotel a new bath house has been under construction for seventeen years but it hasn't been finished because there is no money. Nearby there is a Pioneer House which is 100 years old. There is not enough room for study and the children have to work in the cells of the building.

Not far from the hotel there is a hospital for the party élite and a new building will soon be finished. Two years ago there were rumours that the original committee hotel would be turned into a hospital for children or probably into a Pioneer House. But alas, these were only rumours. Our party élite will never give anything to the people on their own initiative.

Susov, City of Gorky.

ONE of the defenders of Leningrad during the siege of World War Two died not long ago. He was a very respected man.

Eleven war veterans wrote a short obituary. One of them asked the editor of a newspaper in the city of Alexandria in the Kirovograd region to publish it.

The editor answered politely that he could only do so if they got permission from the city's party committee.

Isn't this abominable?

V. Zaitsev, Alexandria, Kirovograd region.

OUR courageous reporters have lashed out at the gargantuan projects to divert Siberian rivers to the south, calling them vanity projects that have no economic value. Meanwhile they have applied to be sent into space in the naïve hope that the hard currency that will have to be found to finance this project will grow on trees.

The behaviour of the Ministry for the Chemical Industry as sponsor is also quite surprising. Instead of focusing on ecology and investing everything available in reducing the enormous scale of pollution from the chemical industry (the facts have been published by the Press) the minister has been trying to win the hearts of the reporting community and of the public by chinking his hard currency as he transfers it from one jacket pocket to another.

Consciously or unconsciously (does it really matter?), they all seek to pass their own ambitions off as those of the State, thus achieving personal gains.

Rather than displaying its over-developed preoccupation with self-prestige and sending people who have nothing to do with space research into space, the Soviet Union would do better to invest its money in a more sensible way and thus earn proper respect.

V. Vasilyev, artist, Kalinin.

ET AL

I found out about my 'statutory rights' as a customer when I decided to buy a motor bike from my neighbour. It turned out that, in order to conclude the deal, we had to travel to Chusovaya (a town in a neighbouring region) to a special shop. At the shop, we were told to apply to the mechanical engineer at the Municipal Services Department for a written assessment of the vehicle's condition. The shop would then value the motor bike on the strength of the assessment. The buyer pays the whole sum to the shop and after three days the previous owner of the vehicle receives it – minus 7 per cent commission! 'What exactly do we pay the shop this 7 per cent for?' I asked. 'Service charge,' was the reply.

What service, may I ask? No one even looked at the motor bike (they don't look at cars either); the written assessment is given solely on the strength of the vehicle's MOT certificate. It would be understandable for the shop to charge a commission fee if it were an agency arranging the whole deal so that one did not have to look for a buyer oneself.

In my opinion, the Council of Ministers' decision is not only against the interests of the individual, particularly in small and remote communities (in large towns there may be a need for these shops), but it is unlawful. I sold my car privately to a neighbour for R6,000, and I still had to pay

R420 'service charge' to a shop where no one even set eyes on my vehicle.

V. Bagatova, Moscow region.

CAN you answer this ticklish question? Why is it in the West they put carpets on the floor and here we hang them on the wall?

T. E. Cheboksari.

I heard that in the Soviet Union it is possible to have sex change operations done. How does one go about getting this done? Please don't ignore this earnest request. I am the father of five daughters. First there were twins. And then triplets were born . . . !

V. N., Tobol Railway Station, Kustanay region.

IN the newspaper *Trud*, I read an article called 'A Big Family' about parents with three children who adopted five girls. This family received a new flat, they bought furniture and many organizations gave them material support. All this seemed to me very humane and reasonable.

I am the mother of seven children. For each child I get seven roubles from the State, but only until the age of five. The disabled of the Great Patriotic War, even those who no longer have their own teeth, are given a kilo of candies by the State on national feast days. I get only 600 grammes for my seven children.

With great difficulty I got a four-roomed flat. To repair it I had to sell my coat. I applied to get some kind of assistance but there was only one response: 'you are to blame that you gave birth to poverty.' I am thinking now that it would be better to tell my children not to give birth but to adopt. Then they will be respected and honoured and will want for nothing. And no one will tell them 'you gave birth to poverty.'

L. Zhmurina, Sverdlovsk.

IT'S a matter of great concern, and it's always in the Press and on television, that our country is over-full of children's orphanages and places of care. We are thirty and have been trying for several years, without success, to have children. We made up our minds to adopt a child and we are now included on the waiting list. Our number is 496. But we know of a married couple with two children who are at exactly the same position as we are on the waiting list. We are concerned that our type of family, childless, has no priority over them.

When we finally get a child for adoption we'll be over forty and people of that age even have grandchildren. Help us.

A. Pancratsiva, Dneypenetrovska.

DO girls aged fifteen and sixteen need such a subject as initial military training at school? Do future mothers need to know how to disassemble and assemble a Kalashnikov? Who had the idea of introducing this into the curriculum? When we graduated from school in the 1960s we didn't have this subject and were none the worse for that. We are no less patriotic and determined to defend our country in an emergency than young people are today.

L. Uzdina, Yaroslavl.

JEWISH people who were decorated during the Great Patriotic War, when emigrating to Israel, have such medals and ribbons taken away by the military committees, as if they were the betrayers of the Motherland. It is not just.

M. Rogavoy, Moscow.

I don't need socialism without beer! I've restructured. I think secretly our leaders have the same opinion.

T. A., Krasnodar.

I heard that in Krasnodar region aliens from outer space have been living there for a whole year. It was written in a local paper. I want to know why the national Press hasn't mentioned a single word of all this?

E. V., Vladimirsk region.

HOW can one understand it? Komsomol *Pravda* published a short article entitled 'Who allowed it?' together with a photograph. Looking at the picture one can't help but notice the striking resemblance between the doll in the picture and our President. I was speechless with astonishment. Our former leaders in the form of matryoshkas [*Russian dolls*] already appear on the counters of co-operatives. One can understand that – but the leading Soviet leaders are turned into matryoshkas by a Japanese firm under the name Gorby, strikingly resembling the original. It's a commercial secret, says the newspaper, who gave permission for the production and sale of these dolls.

In my opinion such a permission could only be given by the owner of the original. Firms pay for such things. If my memory doesn't fail me, the American film star of the sixties, Marilyn Monroe, was paid millions of dollars for giving permission for her vital statistics to be published. And what about the law on the honour and dignity of the President? Probably the Soviet side doesn't see anything humiliating about it. Or maybe it's another way of winning popularity for our President in the world. Of course if the United States sells Bush dolls, France Mitterrand and West Germany Kohl, it means that we shouldn't lag behind the world level of democracy. But the meaning of the word is understood in a very peculiar way.

O. G., Kiev.

ON VE-Day's eve our media broadcast appeals for renewed political reprisals. What are things coming to? We routed a formidable foe in a horrible war – and now we see the vanquished having living standards better than anything we have ever dreamed of. As to our country, its harsh ways killed the people's belief in the State as our protector. If we lived like Germans or the Japanese are now and had prospects like theirs, national separatists would never get strong support in many Soviet republics.

What our country needs is liberty and guaranteed democracy to protect every citizen's right.

A. Morokin, Kaluga.

FOR some reason or other the militia man with his rubber baton has more or less become an expected part of the urban landscape. Paradoxical though it may seem, perestroika has plunged us back into the sad realities of 1966, when we witnessed the first upholders of the law on our streets armed with rubber batons. Between then and now they disappeared, so one might well ask why exactly it is that we need them back again?

Several days ago I was working on a case of non-cooperation with the police, when I came across some documents from two periods – the period of stagnation and the period of perestroika. Both contained the regulations governing use of rubber batons by the militia.

It was very interesting to compare the RSFSR [*Russian*] Ministry of Domestic Affairs decree no. 0030 which was in use in the sixties with its counterpart decree no. 127 dated 6.6.89. I confess I was somewhat confused. In 1966 batons were not to be used against women or the elderly (point three), but nowadays the elderly are no longer exempt, they have been replaced by people with obvious disabilities . . .

Other prohibitions were also changed: whereas point four of the old regulations specifically prohibited blows to the face and head, today's version rather less clearly advises the special services to 'try to avoid hitting the head and neck'.

And there is something else. Why is it that the Soviet Parliament hasn't shown any interest in regulations of this sort? Why did Mr Bakatin [*Interior Minister*] not share the innovations of the 1989 version with the parliamentary delegates? Was he perhaps worried that some of them may voice exactly what they thought about them?

M. Krasovitsky, lawyer, Moscow.

ENCLOSED is a dog registration card issued by the Moscow Dog Owners Club. Apart from breed information, the card must provide data on the dog-owner: name, year of birth, place of work, position, party affiliation. Apparently, the dog-owner's relationship with the Communist party is a major factor when his dog enters competitions. What do you think of that?

Z. H. Kozlova, Moscow.

WE are an average family with average wages. But we have never had any money because our family is large. But in our house there was always joking and laughter. But now misfortune has arrived in a way I never imagined. My children grew up good and industrious. None of them drinks or smokes. All of them worked at different plants then suddenly one of my sons went to work at a co-operative. A dressmaking place. Soon he was earning R450, R500, then R700 and R800 a month. Very expensive things appeared in our house without which we had got along fine for years. The rest of my children still work at their plants where the salaries are R220 – and whatever they do they can't get any more.

So, I asked my son why he received so much money and he answered, 'Well, for instance, if a dress costs twenty roubles we will sell it for forty-five roubles. Our women put a motif on a simple dress and the buyers think it is outstanding.'

Now, my sons, who couldn't imagine living without each other, look at each other like enemies. My 'co-operator' can insult his sisters and brothers any way he likes. I taught my children not to take from anybody else, never to insult or to humiliate anyone. To be honest!

I am a simple worker. During the war I worked on a collective farm. Then I worked twenty years at a plant. My health has been bad in the last few years and my pension is only eighty roubles. But my children never reproached me because I was only able to dress them in a poor way. Probably people will say that I am silly, old, that I should be glad that my son brings the money home. But I have no happiness from such income, because it is from robbery.

For many years the dressmaking shops were run by the State. For whom were such co-operatives created? Why did these dressmakers become robbers of simple working people who have nothing but their honest salary? And this income which they receive in such an easy way only makes them selfish and greedy, money-grabbing. I never thought my son would be so weak. The sun has gone out from our home.

Doesmakava, Sverdlovsk.

43

MY wife and I are both doctors. We have two children. Our joint earnings are R280 a month – R140 each. The minimum requirement for living here according to the Soviet Press is seventy-five roubles per capita per month. Do I need to comment? By comparison a casualty doctor in the USA earns $25,000 a year, a surgeon $125,000. In my opinion the bureaucracy, all of those who get special privileges, are using my family car, are living at my dacha and are eating my family meals!

P. Groosev, Moscow.

I am working in the field of culture. I have worked for more than twenty years and am now at the head of one of the cultural establishments. My wife has had higher education, we have two schoolchildren in senior school and I work very often in the evening and sometimes at the weekend but I don't receive any overtime and no days off in lieu. But that's not what I'm driving at. I've got used to all this. If it's necessary it's necessary. I like my work and that's why I don't consider how much time I spend there. But I don't go very often to theatres or concerts. I have never had a chance in my life to have a rest in a rest home or convalescent home. I'm not well dressed. I have one suit which I've worked in for more than seven years. And as to my overcoat, even longer. I don't have any raincoat, no umbrella and I lack many other necessary things.

I want to mention only one rather important point. I am a subscriber to one or two newspapers and one magazine and of course I would like to subscribe to five times as many. The same applies to my wife and for my children the situation is even worse. With horror I think sometimes if someone in the family dies then we don't have a single kopeck in the bank. There is no money to bury them. If my son or daughter decide they want to get married, what can I do for them? I don't have a single rouble.

At the same time we have millionaires in our country, a lot of rich people. I have come to this conclusion: the higher up a person is, the higher his salary, the more privileges and benefits he has. And where are all the slogans about equality and justice? And how would you understand them now? All of us have got tired of all those beautiful words and mottos which are not supported by reality. We are waiting for beautiful deeds.

A. Ivanov, worker of culture, Belgarat.

PS I have changed my surname on purpose. Judging from what I know our local and regional leadership have not restructured themselves and if I mention my real name there could be trouble.

THE regional management of the Kharkov radio and television has been announcing on local radio for several days that it was starting to work on a self-supporting basis beginning 1 April. In this connection the radio listeners who wanted to congratulate somebody with a song should, together with an application, put a receipt from the bank into the envelope acknowledging that ten roubles has been paid. The question is, is this an April Fool's Day joke or are they really serious? If so, it's much better to go and buy a bottle of vodka with those ten roubles and drink it together with your friend and sing to your heart's content. Or you can go to the Melodia shop and buy a record with the song you or your friend likes and the record only costs three roubles, fifty kopecks. [*If it happens to be among the very few in stock – Ed.*]

B. Paliausky, Kharkov.

Question and Answer

FROM time to time we hear about motor accidents. Does anyone know how many accidents there are per year and where?

M. Mukhin, Khabarovsk.

The State Automobile Inspectorate answers:

In 1989 there were 319,557 traffic accidents reported in the Soviet Union involving 58,651 deaths and 347,402 injured. This was a rise of 16.9 per cent compared with 1988, with a rise in the death rate of 24.3 per cent and injured 16.7 per cent.

These are the highest figures since the introduction of the motor car into the Soviet Union. And they are on the increase in all the republics. Armenia, Byelorussia, Moldavia, the Ukraine and the Russian Federation have particularly dangerous roads.

The main reasons for accidents on the roads are non-observance of the Highway Code by drivers (78.5 per cent), and by pedestrians (23.9 per cent), as well as the poor condition of many roads and highways (10.9 per cent), and people driving vehicles unfit for use on the public highway.

It has been shown that 48.3 per cent of accidents involving death and injury occur in built-up areas. The relevant figures for death and injury are 18,113 and 165,919 respectively. The number of accidents has risen most sharply in Ashkhabad, Kishinev, Kiev and Riga.

In 1989 it was reported that 78.5 per cent of all motor accidents were caused by drivers, involving 83.7 per cent of all deaths and 82.2 per cent of all injuries on the roads.

Taking motor accidents caused by drivers alone, we find that 27.1 per cent involve State-owned vehicles, 67.9 per cent involve private transport, in 7.3 per cent of cases ownership of the vehicle has not been recorded and 0.6 per cent of vehicles were owned by co-operatives or other independent organizations.

Last year the drivers of public transport were responsible for 67,950 road accidents (+7.6 per cent), causing 17,169 (+19.5 per cent) deaths and 76,875 (+6.8 per cent) injured.

Safety on public transport is a major headache. In 1988 bus drivers were responsible for 7,448 (+6.9 per cent) of all road accidents involving 1,514 (+20.4 per cent) deaths and 10,770 (+5.8 per cent) injured. It is not uncommon to find that the drivers of public transport do not even have driving licences (818 road accidents − 11 per cent of all accidents caused by bus drivers).

Every fourth (23.9 per cent) accident is caused by pedestrians. In one year alone there were 76,503 (+17.3 per cent) accidents caused by pedestrians, involving 79,379 (+17.5 per cent) deaths and injuries. Of this number 15,359 accidents (+31.7 per cent) were caused by people under the influence of alcohol.

The rate of injuries to children on the roads remains high.

In the last year 5,584 (+11.4 per cent) of children under sixteen died and 47,992 (+17.4 per cent) were injured on the roads. Of these, 61.2 per cent were pedestrians and 24 per cent were passengers.

Additional information on crime rates:

Comparative crime rates for premeditated murder in the USSR and the USA over the last ten years.

| | USA | | USSR | |
| | | Per 100,000 | | Per 100,000 |
Year	Thsnd	population	Thsnd	population
1979	21.5	9.7	20.9	8.0
1980	23.0	10.4	21.4	8.1
1981	22.5	9.8	21.3	8.0
1982	21.0	9.1	21.5	7.9
1983	19.3	8.3	21.3	7.8
1984	18.7	7.9	20.5	7.5
1985	19.0	7.9	18.7	6.8
1986	20.6	8.6	14.8	5.3
1987	20.1	8.3	14.7	5.2
1988	Figures not available		16.7	5.9

As is well known there are a whole range of acts which are punishable under administrative law in the USSR but which come under criminal law in the USA. Apart from that, grievous bodily harm causing death is treated as murder in the USA, whereas in the USSR it is categorized as premeditated grevious bodily harm.

The main thing, however, that should be preoccupying both countries is not who has the most of whatever sort of murders etc., but the reasons for these crimes, and what can be done about them.

A. Shestak, candidate of juridical sciences.

THE rumour is that the police have stopped taking people to court for staying away from work. Is it true?

G. Skalnikov, Smolensk.

A. Petrov answers:

Statistics on convictions for a parasitical way of life – sentences already in effect (thousands of people). Type of crime: vagrancy, begging, staying away from work (not earning one's keep).

Total number for the following years:

1980	'81	'82	'83	'84	'85	'86	'87	'88
53.6	58.1	60.2	69.2	76.8	63.9	31.9	9.7	1.9

including for not earning one's keep:

1980	'81	'82	'83	'84	'85	'86	'87	'88
27.5	37.8	41.4	49.4	56.9	47.6	24.2	7.1	1.1

The overall number of convictions was five hundred over the first six months of 1989 including three hundred for not earning one's keep.

The overall number of people convicted in the Russian Federation on the basis of Article 209 of the Penal Code of the Russian Federation (vagrancy, begging, not earning one's keep) amounted to 1,000 in 1988.

The information was made available by the USSR Ministry of Justice.

Prior to 1989 these statistics were strictly classified. There are no grounds for assuming that the number of vagrants, beggars and spongers has decreased. Apparently, they have become a lower priority with the authorities.

Additional information on pensions:

IN 1988 the government paid out R55 billion in pensions and benefits. Benefit was received by 58.6 million people – 43 million were Old Age Pensioners, 6.5 million were disabled and 5.7 million were widows.

The minimum pension received by retired manual and white-collar workers has remained at the 1981 level of R50 a month. Retired collective farmers received an increase in 1985 from R28 to R40 per month. Pensions allotted ten or more years ago have been increased above these minima. Manual and white-collar workers received R55 a month from 1985 and collective farmers R50 from 1988. Of the forty-one million people living below the minimum subsistence level, one-fifth are pensioners.

Number of pensioners receiving minimum pension rate (figures for the end of the year).

| | In millions | | % of OAPs | |
	1985	1988	1985	1988
Manual and white-collar workers	2.7	1.8	8.9	5.4
Collective farmers	5.2	5.7	58.4	61.2

THERE was a television interview the other day with a homosexual who described how it was that he had become corrupted in his youth. I've heard that under new criminal legislation homosexuality is no longer going to be treated as a crime. Since it is the militia who have to deal with this in their daily working lives, I would like to know what they think about it.

K. Vorotnikova, Pushchino, Moscow district.

V. Kachanov, Moscow Criminal Department, Department of Sexual Crimes, answers:

As the law now stands, homosexuality is a criminal offence throughout the Soviet Union. In Moscow there are only about ten or twelve criminal proceedings brought against minors for homosexual activity per year (Art. 121, p. 11, RSFSR Criminal Code), although there are more cases than this that do not reach the courts. Homosexuals corrupt the morals of children and poison them psychologically for ever. This is the greatest danger. For the most part homosexuals are people suffering from innate or developing psychological predisposition to sexual deviations.

Every year between 15–20,000 serious crimes against homosexuals are recorded in Moscow, crimes such as murder, gang attacks and mugging. The victims and their friends are not usually very willing to co-operate with the police and many of the attacks go unreported because they are frightened of getting their friends involved in any subsequent investigation. Yet in many cases these attacks are ferocious and carefully planned.

It is well known that Aids and venereal diseases are spread by homosexual activity.

However, the law does not regard all unconventional contacts between men as homosexuality. For example, certain extreme acts committed against a young girl are regarded in law as 'perverted rape' whereas the same acts committed against a young boy are regarded as 'corrupt acts'. The penalties differ, but the consequences for the victims are always the same – psychological and physical trauma. Parents, who for reasons of false modesty do not report these incidents, are acting against the interests of their children and of society, and actually helping the criminals.

In 1989 the Moscow Criminal Department's Sex Crimes Squad was abolished, regardless of the fact that these crimes need to be dealt with by specialized officers.

In comparison with Western Europe, the Soviet Union doesn't have the resources to fund the medical and social programmes needed to defend society from these people. That is why we want to retain existing legislation against homosexuality, to act as a deterrent, especially in cases of rape and crimes against minors.

If we were to totally abolish this legislation we would be left without the means of punishing those who corrupt the morals of our children.

IN his reply to a letter sent in by Mrs Vorotnikova, Mr Kachanov of the Moscow Criminal Department speaks out against the abolition of Article 121 of the RSFSR Criminal Code on homosexuality, since, in his opinion, this would leave children and young people at risk. I would like to put forward a different point of view.

Firstly: laws to defend minors against corruption of sexual morals by anybody of any age or sex exist in all countries, and nobody is suggesting they be repealed in the USSR. Heterosexual acts of this kind are no less harmful than homosexual, and the same standards should apply as is the case in the vast majority of civilized countries.

The only legislation that should be changed is that affecting homosexual relations between consenting adults. One cannot help wondering what the logic is behind our present law which prohibits homosexual relations between men but ignores lesbianism among women.

Secondly: according to Mr Kachanov, 'homosexuals are people suffering from innate or developing psychological predisposition to sexual deviations.' If this were so then these people should not be punished but should be given treatment. However, experience elsewhere shows that homosexuals are different to the majority of people only by virtue of their sexual orientation, and that in everything else they are exactly the same. There is no basis for considering them either psychologically or socially inferior.

It is a blatant breach of human rights to discriminate against and persecute homosexuals, and this was recognized by lawyers the world over in 1964. Some countries have legislated against discrimination.

Thirdly: according to Mr Kachanov 'homosexuals corrupt the morals of children and poison them psychologically for ever. This is the greatest danger.' Again, experience in the rest of the world shows that the percentage of paedophiles, that is people who are sexually attracted to children, is the same among homosexuals as it is among heterosexual men, and that aggressive behaviour and rape is far more common among the latter.

Criminal violence in homosexual circles is generally committed by heterosexual men as a way of asserting their power. The same is true of teenagers among whom the first homosexual experience is more likely to be with their peers rather than something forced upon them by adults.

Fourthly: Mr Kachanov very properly indicates the woolly legal definition of many sex crimes, but at the same time he is confusing sexual violence and seduction when he states that 'the consequences for the victims are always the same – psychological and physical trauma.' In actual fact he is talking about two separate things and the psychological ramifications are very different, and not the same for each individual. Unfortunately, Soviet doctors and psychologists are not trained to deal with people in these situations and investigation by unqualified people can often prove worse for the child than the original experience itself. This is the real reason why some parents decide not to go to the police, thus letting the perpetrators off scot-free. It has nothing to do with false modesty.

Fifthly: while Mr Kachanov is eager to make play of the link between homosexuality and venereal diseases and Aids, everyone else realizes that this is not the only, nor even the main source of these diseases. As for the difficulties in investigating crimes against homosexuals who 'are frightened of getting their friends involved', I would strongly suggest that it is not the gay community who are to blame but rather the outdated Criminal Code. Who in their right mind would squeal on themselves? The first step in the fight against Aids has to be the abolition of Article 121 – there are plenty of other Articles in the Criminal Code protecting children and minors of both sexes.

Mr Kachanov is quite right in saying that only specially trained officers should be put on to cases involving sex crimes. The sad fact is, and this is supported by his letter, the Moscow Criminal Department are not sufficiently trained in this area. Nobody is arguing that the law shouldn't protect people from sexual violence or children from corruption of morals. Of course it should. But playing on old fears and ridiculous stereotypes is not the way to go about it. We've got enough of those as it is.

I. Kon, Associate of USSR Academy of Pedagogical Sciences
and the International Academy of Sexology.

CHAPTER TWO

NATIONALITY AND CULTURE

*The interests of socialism are above
the interests of the rights of nations
to self-determination.*
— Lenin

*Ethnic and national unrest has riven the Soviet Union in the last
three years. More than 100 nationalities live in the fifteen
republics of the country: Russian Federation, Ukraine, Byelorussia, Uzbekistan, Kazakhstan, Georgia, Azerbaijan, Lithuania,
Moldavia, Latvia, Kirgizia, Tajikistan, Armenia, Turkmenia and
Estonia. In 1989 the population of the USSR was 286,731,000,
an increase of twenty-four million – 9 per cent – on 1979. The
population grew in all the republics with the highest rates in
Uzbekistan (+ 29 per cent), Tajikistan (+ 34 per cent) and Turkmenia (+ 27 per cent). Russia and Estonia are the most urbanized
republics with, respectively, 74 per cent and 72 per cent living in
towns. By contrast, in the Central Asian republics and Moldavia
less than half the populations live in cities or towns.*

THE government's treatment of Lithuania has upset me a
great deal. Why should we hold it against them that they
want to live well, better than we do? They may even succeed.
They should be given our blessing and not be hindered all the
time. All our republics have the right to self-determination.

Why should this right be abused? In Uzbekistan they even have their own president. And they are doing fine. Perhaps better than we do. It can't be right to always act on someone else's bidding.

Not long ago, I happened to buy *Komsomolskaya Pravda* [*young communists' newspaper*] and read an article about American farmers. You may not believe me, but I burst into tears. Why is their life so good, so easy? And everything is so clean and tidy. Here, in Russia, we are forever shifting manure or other rubbish; there – machines do everything.

And the abundance of food! Fifty kinds of milk. I often have to trudge to the shops several times in one day to catch the delivery. Even when I manage to buy milk, it more often than not turns out unfit for human consumption and my cat gets it. The same with sausages. What do we eat then? Not much. There is little food, and it's poor quality. Our freshwater fish smell and taste of chemicals. How are we supposed to live? There are never-ending talks in Moscow. Lithuania is being blamed, it appears, for wanting to improve its standard of living. They have decided to put perestroika in action, not on paper. Why should anyone want to stop them? It was our respected president, Mikhail Gorbachev, who first started perestroika, and now what? I remember when he first travelled throughout the country, like Tsar Peter I, to see for himself how people lived. Then he decided to restructure the country. Now, it seems, his only worry is that he'll have a government of ministers without portfolios.

I don't know how you, in Moscow, live. We have a serious food shortage, and the crime rate is high. Life is hard for us ordinary mortals. Only empty words. First we were waiting for the Congress of People's Deputies. Now we are waiting for the twenty-eighth Party Congress. And then what? A deadlock. It doesn't even bear to think about our country's ecology. What will the future bring for the next generation, as yet unborn? There is no peace in our souls, only heartache.

Stebekova, Tyumen.

ONE of the most serious obstacles preventing us from reaching a successful solution to the nationality issue in our country is the long practice of official and compulsory nationality registration of every Soviet citizen on the basis of his 'biological' or 'genetic' characteristics. This system, which arbitrarily creates rigid and immutable ethnic boundaries between Soviet people, can be justified neither by scientific and theoretical nor by political considerations.

In scientific theory, concepts of 'nationality', 'nation' or 'ethnic' are social concepts, not biological ones. At least, such is the Marxist point of view, as opposed to the nationalistic one. Accordingly, the nationality of each individual citizen should be defined by social, and not biological, conditions. A human being is not born a representative of a certain nation: he or she becomes one in the course of his or her life, developing and forming as an individual being.

From the political point of view, the practice of determining one's nationality on a biological basis threatens the most elementary rights of the individual, let alone any rights that may be given to individuals of certain nationalities.

The CPSU Draft Programme for the twenty-eighth Party Congress contains a section (in the chapter entitled 'Towards a New Federation') with the heading The Rights of the Nation and the Rights of the Individual. Unfortunately, while the rights of the nation are properly defined, the rights of the individual have been given only nominal consideration.

Therefore, we propose introducing an alteration to this section of the Draft Programme by adding an introductory paragraph as follows: 'Citizens of the USSR shall have the right to determine and choose freely their nationality. National status should become a matter of personal choice for each individual citizen. Any violation of ethnic freedom of the Soviet people shall be legally punishable.

'Soviet citizens shall also have the right to choose their national language and culture.'

In view of the present situation in the Soviet Union, we believe that such a move is a vital measure.

K. Zachesov, Associate Professor and Doctor of Philosophy;
Z. Kadiev, Associate Professor and Doctor of Philosophy;
N. Gasanov, Associate Professor and Doctor of Philosophy.

(On each form a citizen fills in the fifth question – Item 5 – is on nationality – Ed.)

I am deeply convinced that to begin the restructuring of our national relations it is necessary to cancel Item 5, indications of nationality, as it seems like an underwater rock on which many human beings face disaster. This item is, in many cases, one of the most decisive factors with employers over whether they hire you or not, whether to admit you to higher education institutions, whether to promote you or not.

Even before a child is born the mother is asked about her nationality and the father's. Does this question determine whether the birth is successful or not? I'm the mother of two children, am I missing something very important here? When a baby becomes a child he or she belongs to a nationality about which he or she understands little. The nationality of acquaintances is of no interest to the child.

The first time the child does become aware of it is at school where the class register has nationality against his or her surname. What for? I'm a teacher myself and I know that no one evaluates or relates education and intelligence among nationalities. But it has become a custom. It is not by chance that at school we are witnessing the first stirrings of national hostilities.

If you want to become a student or if you want to borrow books from the library, or to become an employee – or if you want to take your dog for training – you have to indicate your nationality. Our laws and the constitution outlaw discrimination, so why does this exist? If we believe that the basis of it is the principle of Soviet ethnographic science then isn't it the case that whether a person belongs to this or that nationality is determined not by some objective natural principle but by his or her self-awareness. A human being belongs to the nationality with which he thinks himself inseparably connected by the common language, by culture and by his spiritual life.

M. Shutalova, teacher, Kharkov.

(To qualify for a minimum state pension women must have worked for twenty years and men twenty-five. But to induce people to work in inhospitable climes the State has sometimes made some unholy bargains – Ed.)

WHY is it that for the native population of the north the calculation for a working year for pension entitlement is one year while for those that have arrived in this region to work one year it is calculated as eighteen months?

With the indigenous population the large enterprises don't give such privileged deals. Sometimes, when we are looking for the reasons for national conflict, they are even enshrined in our laws.

I have been working here in Yarkutsia [*a diamond mining area*] for twenty-eight years. My children were brought up here. Nearby a local man is doing the same work as I am but his working life is considered to be of lower value than mine. Who has invented all this?

G. Tshen-Shan, Nyzhneyansk, northern republic.

(State planning still rules agriculture, particularly the collective farms. Often, the crops to be sown reflect national shortage rather than suitability for the land – Ed.)

I respect all nations. However, I am watching the current events in our republics and I'm horrified. There are strikes, calls for secession and I know that all of them are living much better than, for example, we in Kaluga and the rest of the Russian Federation. In Russia the death rate is higher, the state of the economy is lower and culture is in stagnation.

If we judge by the situation in our town then the citizens of the Russian Federation are like national minorities. I consider myself to be deprived, to be without a voice – a person who can't change anything. But the representatives of national minorities from the south, for example, are feeling at home in Kaluga, even enjoying a feeling of superiority. They have money – and we? They have nationality solidarity – do we have it? They have mandarin gardens and greenhouses, flats, cars, vodka – and what do I have personally: my work and a 20.8-square-metre apartment for five people and my faith in the future fast running out.

I was surprised by the last plenum on agriculture which everyone was waiting for – nothing new. The only thing more horrible, more terrible than the situation we have in our collective farms in our region would be nuclear war! Now, under administrative instruction, we are sowing wheat which will not grow here. We stake everything on good weather and good crops. And I think a peasant should be the owner of his land. He should grow what will actually grow in our region. He would change to flax, which is in demand, which we can sell to get good wheat from the Ukraine and Georgian oranges. Both us and the State would benefit.

I don't understand our laws too well. But if they are the same for all the people then I can't understand why people who don't come to work aren't dismissed, how it's possible in other republics to go on strike for months and not to be fined. I think it's high time we thought seriously about the Russian unfertile lands and how to sow crops to suit them. And it's high time we all realized just how bad things are.

V. Makarov, Kaluga.

IN the twenties and thirties I studied and then I worked in the mines. I have always been an internationalist. In the past, whatever problems arose, no one ever blamed the people for their different nationalities. Nobody even felt the influence of his nationality on his relations with other nationalities. The same international spirit flourished during the years of the war in the military college where I studied and at the Front.

Only in 1943, when I was a prisoner of the Germans in Austria, did I come across for the first time the cultivation of nationalism. The military prisoners of different nationalities were separated from each other by wires and separate compounds. And Russian people were even separated from the Ukrainian people. Here for the first time I listened to how the people on one side of a wire shouted insults at others.

This division was required by German fascism and they succeeded in all this. And in such an advanced, cultured country as Germany of the thirties, fascism achieved victory by appealing to the innate nationalism of the worst elements of the German people whose numbers were great enough to take power in the absence of any real opposition. In our country, as in fascist Germany, the attempts to sow national conflicts in many regions are enjoying success. We have even killed and wounded each other.

No one is fighting us now. We are not occupied but thousands of the Soviet people have become refugees, their houses burned, their property robbed. There are pogroms in the republics. Doesn't the Supreme Soviet understand that under the shelter of international relations an anti-Soviet campaign is being unleashed with the purpose of weakening our system?

V. Yanovski, Nyeprepitrovsk.

WHEN our State was being created a blunder was made – we shouldn't have given the republics within the USSR their national names. And now we mustn't worsen the situation. We must strive for the disappearance, gradually, not by force, of nationality as an official parameter of a citizen. Look around. Is nationality mentioned in the documents of other countries? Do many countries have national territorial divisions? See what it leads to in such countries as Yugoslavia.

The Russian language should not be imposed as the State language and people should not be divided into national groups. It is necessary to raise the status of territories but deputies should not be counted in accordance with their nationalities.

Olevsky, Magetagorsk.

AFTER the Second World War all Soviet miners were awarded the medal 'For Valiant Labour during the Great Patriotic War in 1941–45' for their selfless work during time of war.

The only exceptions were miners who were ethnic Germans.

Why is it that the authorities have not yet undone this injustice committed in the Stalin era?

O. Gurr, Angren, Tashkent region.

WE need to find a radical solution to the nationalities problem in the USSR and this solution should be based on the ideas put forward by Lenin in the first party programme, where it was stated that nations should 'have the right to self-determination, even to the point of separating and creating independent states'. Today this right is either simply overlooked or glossed over in embarrassed silence. Yet it was this very right that Lenin and the party carried with them into the October Revolution. It was this very right that enabled Finland to separate and set up as an independent state.

Nowadays the peoples of the Baltic republics and Moldavia are clearly and inspiringly working towards independence. Not simply independence, but they want to leave the USSR altogether. They have this right, so why shouldn't they use it? The usual argument put forward against using it is that their economies are too closely intertwined with the USSR economy. Nobody, however, is suggesting that this should not continue to be so. They have no choice but to continue to be economically interdependent even after political independence, otherwise they will soon be bankrupt. Most of their raw materials come from the USSR.

If we really do want to build a common European home in deeds and not just words, and if by this we mean a place in which free nations can live together on a free and equal basis, while being members of a single economy, then granting full state independence to nations has to be one of the basic conditions for founding this home. Each republic that wants to be part of this home must be able to do so as an independent sovereign state, which will then become one of the independent national apartments in the general European home, on an equal footing with France, Belgium, Luxembourg, Spain and other apartments already established in the home.

It must also be on a level footing with Hungary, Bulgaria, Czech, Slovakia, Poland and other East European countries, which have not yet joined.

R. Mikhailov, historian, Moscow.

WRITING to you are mothers of frontier guards doing their military service in the Lenkoran unit. In fact, they are hostages of two peoples – the Armenians and the Azerbaijanis – involved in a conflict. Please explain to us why this conflict should be resolved at the cost of the health and lives of our children? We and they do not need the land of Armenia or Azerbaijan. Wouldn't it be better to have volunteers do the job?

Nikitenko, Romanova, Molova, Mamiyeva and Matsukhova, Nalchik.

THE council of ministers of the Estonian Republic took a decision banning the sending of parcels containing practically all kinds of consumer goods. Post offices opened the parcels and many people had to return home with them. My parents live in another republic and it is my duty to help them. I can visit them only once or twice a year and now I am not allowed to help them. Naturally it is humiliating to go to shops with coupons to buy sugar but it is more humiliating not to have the right to use this sugar the way you want.

According to the new decrees I cannot send it to my mother who is fond of making jam. As for the parcels sent to the people of Estonia there is no banning or limits. It means that my old mother can send a present to me but I cannot send a present to her for her birthday. Isn't it monstrous?

We are equal in this State, however it appears that the people living in Estonia have more rights than the rest of the people living in other republics. One has the impression that our management has found a very primitive and humiliating way of raising the living standards of the people of Estonia.

E. Grigoreva, Koghtla Yarva.

(*This is happening more often throughout the republics. A seismologist I met who spends most of his year in Tajikistan, who has a house there and whose family was brought up in the republic, is banned, like others, from bringing fruit from his garden to Moscow or even jam. And a juice extractor he took there was expropriated – Ed.*)

THE events going on in Lithuania are the focus of attention of all of the people in the Soviet Union – but so many men, so many minds. Some people call the Lithuanians ungrateful brutes, or even fascists. Others think that they are doing the right thing. In such cases the law should play the key role. According to the constitution of the USSR, article 70, every nation has the right to self-determination and according to article 72, every nation, every republic has the right to leave the USSR. These articles should be the basis of solving all national and territorial problems. We should remember Lenin's warning: the constitution becomes fiction when the law and reality contradict each other.

Zuyev, Severodvinsk.

TRAVEL

RECENTLY there have been many articles about the international post. In all of these the authorities deny that the secret services are examining international mail. But my case disproves that. Recently I received one letter and a postcard. To my great surprise, when I opened the envelope, I found eight more air mail letters inside which were addressed to the USA. All of these were stamped by Kiev Post Office. On my envelope the stamp was 10 December. The stamps on the other letters were 11 December, a day later. Evidently, during the examination and reading of my letter somebody mistakenly included the other people's letters with mine.

O. Helms, USSR citizen (living in West Germany).

(Photostats of the eight USA-bound letters were provided – Ed.)

WHEN I arrived from Italy where I had been working and had lots of good friends I decided to send a parcel to them. After thinking about what was best I decided a Russian samovar and a set of souvenir wooden kitchen utensils would symbolize something purely Russian but at the post office it appeared that there was a list of things which could not be sent to capitalist countries. After reading it I understood that I couldn't send anything. I was at a loss because I just couldn't believe that in the time of perestroika a samovar and kitchen utensils were equal to drugs or weapons.

Shakmin, City of Volshky.

WHEN you go to the post office to collect a small parcel from abroad, you have to pay a ninety-kopeck customs duty. A few years ago, this 'service charge' was only twelve kopecks. For a slightly bigger package, you pay R2.95. Also, when you send a parcel abroad, you have to pay customs duty. I am not against customs officers checking the contents of parcels received or sent abroad, but why should I pay for it? Tourists do not pay for customs clearance! We don't pay for baggage checks when we board a plane. The practice of paying customs duties at the post office should be stopped and other ways of replenishing the national budget devised. Such as increasing the number of trips abroad for Soviet citizens, and encouraging more foreign tourists to visit the USSR.

D. Alekseev, Cheboksary.

NOT long ago I received a present from the United States. Its price was about $40, or $\frac{1}{60}$ of the average monthly pay of an American worker. I'm a worker too. But $\frac{1}{60}$ of my pay is four roubles. Customs duties cost me R160, or $\frac{40}{60}$ of my pay. Not bad, eh?

Why this devaluation of the rouble? Well it has value there (in the West). But here (in the Soviet Union) I live on this rouble and this is my life, good or bad. Do I deserve this humiliation? Why should a working man pay such gargantuan duties? This is a moral humiliation. I believe there must be reasonable limits. I don't understand either why we have to pay customs duties for goods which are in acute shortage in this country. Take razor blades, for example. I have to pay customs duties to the State because the State can't provide me with essential goods. Why?

V. Bochkarev, Voronezh.

UNLIKE some of your correspondents who only came across customs regulations at Shermetyevo (Moscow international airport), I considered myself fortunate. Before setting off for Australia to visit my mother and brother I not only read the regulations but even copied them down. They were exactly as related to *AIF* by the deputy head of customs N. Lyutov, i.e. it is allowable to bring into the USSR one item of each type of radio and video equipment without paying duty.

However, on my return I found things are very different in practice. Duty was imposed on all but one television set. Moreover, duty was based on current prices in the Soviet Union. As a result my video machine cost me $299 in Australia – and a further R500 in the USSR. The total duty imposed on all my other purchases at the official exchange rate amounted to R2,586.

How could I be expected to have that kind of money on me at the customs in Moscow when I live in Chelyabinsk? I left my goods in store and set about taking out a loan, most of my savings having gone on the trip. The ticket was expensive, I needed money for currency and for presents for my family. While I was collecting the money to pay the duty some time had elapsed. As a result I was obliged to pay a further 729 roubles for storage costs. My total debt amounted to R3,500.

In three years I will be retiring. Will I ever be able to settle with my creditors before I die? I earn only R230–250 a month. I have not written to my relatives in Australia. I am too ashamed. They will say – and rightly too – that our State is 'stripping' its own people.

Would I have gone to all the trouble of bringing back a video and cassettes, a jacket and sports shirts and half a kilo of coffee if these things were freely available in our own shops at acceptable prices?

B. Yashenkov, Chelyabinsk.

AIF gives much coverage to the problems of Soviet citizens leaving the Soviet Union and coming back. You mention clever decrees and decisions on the question. But all this is just window dressing, nothing more. I'll give you an example. Last March I got an invitation from the United States. It was declared that the formalities would be reduced to one month and that those going to visit the United States would get R200 worth of hard currency. In fact, the formalities took two months as before. As for the exchange, it was limited to R200. It was also declared that there was no increase in the cost of tickets by Aeroflot. Nevertheless, the price rose by

R500. It was also declared that one could go abroad without any invitation, but in fact the Council of Ministers of the USSR banned all kinds of trips because it was decided to sell tickets only in hard currency.

It's unthinkable. If you want to visit your relatives both in the United States and Canada you have got to fly to the United States and then come back and then fly to Canada. Isn't it humiliating? Now we're talking about the disappearance of cheap goods – as for Aeroflot, cheap tickets just disappear. Their economic incompetence and the fact that Aeroflot failed in its joint venture with Pan American compelled them to find a way out of the situation. They found it. They put the currency problems on the shoulders of the Soviet people.

Tolchinsky, Moscow.

WE talk a lot about the liberty of people but sometimes we don't realize that Stalin's laws are still in action. Sometimes they may not be noticeable: they may be on paper but they are stronger than steel. I have a sister living abroad, across the sea. We haven't seen each other for fifty years. And I can't visit her despite appearing to have the right to.

The point is that my children have access to what is said to be terribly top secret information at their enterprise, which is backward compared to modern technology.

Whenever I express to the authorities my wish to see my ill sister before one of us dies, my children don't sleep because they are frightened that this will have an effect on them at work as those who join these top secret plants fill in questionnaires on things like whether there is any correspondence with relatives living abroad, through many generations – let alone speaking about trips there.

I'm not mistaken when I say that the family of an American designer and inventor of strategic arms travelled throughout the whole world. Isn't it high time we had a reasonable approach to all this? There should be only one person responsible for keeping secrets, the person to whom they were entrusted.

Vinitza.

I was invited to visit Denmark as a guest. In Kiev I was given a questionnaire and I would call it a masterpiece of bureaucracy. Point two asks me about my nationality, point six demands that I should mention absolutely all my relatives. But the most interesting was point seven. It reads 'your working activity in the last fifteen years. Mention all the places of work and their addresses'. It's hard for me, a pensioner, to remember all those addresses and what use is this? I believe it's high time to reconsider all those questionnaires.

Of course, one of my answers in point seven was not quite true to fact and so my departure to Denmark was put off.

Greenberg, Kiev.

IN the middle of 1984, Sebastopol was designated a border zone. The fact was not revealed by the Press. God knows why this decision was taken. Maybe the city is full of spies? Or maybe the tourists who come to Sebastopol try to swim to foreign countries across the Black Sea? Now you can visit the city only if you have a pass. You must have an invitation from Sebastopol, as if you were going abroad, and you aren't allowed to take more than two children with you. It's necessary to write to the man in charge of the passport department and then you will have to wait for two or three weeks. Then your loyalty will be checked and according to the instructions of the KGB your pass will be valid for thirty days.

My great-grandfather took part in the defence of Sebastopol in 1854–55. My grandfather took part in the uprising with Lieutenant Schmidt and my mother was a participant in the defence of Sebastopol in 1941 and '42. I was born in Sebastopol and I grew up in it and now have two grown-up children and eight grandchildren. So you can appreciate our difficulties if we decide to visit our relatives in Sebastopol.

Maybe the fathers of the city decided to isolate Sebastopol from the rest of the country to have better food supplies. Well, the situation in the city is just the same as anywhere else. The citizens have coupons for butter, tea, soap, detergent and other goods. So a special isolated place has not been created. Maybe the border is diligently guarded and no one can get to Sebastopol without a pass, but according to the local Press in the markets there are lots of people who come to the city without any pass. This idea by the city fathers has cost our State a pretty penny – lots of milita, crews checking passes, people writing out permissions, and so on and so forth.

Laxinko, retired colonel, Moscow.

SOME years ago the customs regulations were added to by one item, as a result of which an amendment was made concerning the luggage of generals of the Soviet Army and admirals of the marine fleet. This means that the personal luggage of generals and admirals when they go abroad and on their return to the USSR is not subjected to customs control, unlike everyone else's. What is the reason for this change in the rules? Is it because all of them without exception are honest and unselfish, or could it be something else? Perhaps because generals and admirals carry in their luggage items and documents which contain State secrets?

G. Rucusuyev, Leningrad.

ON 2 February I together with my colleague S. Shigedev were due to come back from Saratov to Moscow by Aeroflot flight no. 762. The captain was pilot first-class Klimenov. One hundred and seventeen passengers took their seats in the aircraft and at 4 p.m. we were supposed to take off. However, the plane did not take off and no reasons were given. We waited for half an hour, then one hour while other planes took off, although by then the crew and the airport management had told us that the weather forecasts were bad for flying. One hour and a half later, with the best three seats in the plane empty, a black Volga car pulled up alongside the plane and two men and a woman got out and took these three seats. Later we found out that our flight had been postponed by the leaders of the Saratov regional party committee of the CPSU who were in a hurry to go to Moscow.

Our aircraft began to taxi up the runway but the snow started to fall and a mist came in. The passengers were then taken back to the terminal. Can you imagine the reaction of the passengers to this, especially those with small children and those in transit through Moscow? One hundred and seventeen people had to spend nineteen hours in the over-crowded airport and eventually arrived in Moscow in the middle of the night. The party leadership of the region, however, went straight from the aircraft to a Volga car and then went to Moscow by train in sleeping carriages.

A. Kurganov, Moscow.

AT the beginning of this month I happened to see off my relatives who were leaving for the Federal Republic of Germany. Now I know how hard it is, I will not speak about bureaucracy because there is a lot of it everywhere in this country. I will touch on the problem of savings. Most of those who are leaving the Soviet Union are over forty. They had something here, houses, cars, and it's not a secret that among Soviet Germans the standard of living is above average. So they sell everything and get quite a big sum of money which they cannot take with them.

But it's not their fault that the Soviet rouble is not convertible. And they start buying expensive goods, and they pay threefold for them. Some co-operatives supply them with black-market goods.

By the way, very strange word combinations can be seen in our Soviet Press. Soviet Germans, Ethnic Germans – why not simply Germans? Why are there no Soviet Armenians or Ethnic Lithuanians? It is trifling, of course, but back to the money problem which is more serious. Why is it that the roubles go neither to the government nor to the relatives but to speculators who get some goods and sell them at sky-high prices?

When Germans arrive in Moscow they are met with tourist buses and they are charged R2,000 for an hour's drive. Four families pay R500 each. It costs R100 to enter the embassy. In a nutshell, I'd like the institutions involved in this business to change their attitudes to the Germans leaving the Soviet Union so that the Germans will not spit when they think of this country. I am still a Soviet German aged twenty-three.

B.K., Yermak.

THE PAST

THE Politiszdat (State political publishing house) plans to start publication of a book *From Reality to Revelation* and this will consist of scientific comment on different parts of the Old and New Testaments. This will be aimed at scientists and specialists with a planned circulation of 200,000 copies. Why is it not possible for the same publishing house to publish the Bible as it is? The Bible is a monument of world culture and everyone should get acquainted with it in its original form, as it is, not with comments on it from 'experts'; anyone who is interested in culture, history and philosophy. In many works of Western literature and also in the works of our classic writers there are a lot of quotations from the Bible, both on everyday life and the life of God. Our modern readers, let alone our writers and journalists, haven't yet had an opportunity to get acquainted with the Bible, to read it and to appreciate to the full its advantages and disadvantages. How long is it going to continue that there is only the chance for us to get to know it through secondary sources and to get only crumbs from the table of the world's cultural heritage?

Biblical criticism is rather widely published in our country but it's impossible to get hold of the object of criticism. From an ethical point of view that is indefensible. The Bible was used as the creative stimulus of the masterpieces of world culture – of paintings, of music and of literature. There are so many that I can't begin to mention them.

B. Olchin, a member of the union of journalists, Ivanovo.

(*The Bible is published only by the Russian Orthodox Church and because of paper shortages and because the ownership of the means of production – all large printing presses – is in the hands of the party, circulation is small. The result is a black market in Bibles. Inside one of the holiest places in Russia, the monastery complex of Zagorsk, you can watch black marketeers – in beards and long hair mimicking the priesthood – attempt to sell copies of the Bible to the faithful for huge prices – Ed.*)

I was born into the family of a peasant. During the years of the war together with other honest citizens of the country I tried to defend the Soviet Motherland. I am a believer of the Russian Orthodox Church and I always prayed to God to crush fascism so that after the victory I could come home safe and sound. My prayers came true and I came back home.

After the war I helped to improve the power of our State. I worked hard on my collective farm despite the wounds inflicted by a fascist bullet. I visited the church and prayed that the terrible years of the war would never happen again. When I became sixty-eight years old I felt that I was exhausted as I have always done physical work. So I retired. Then the authorities of our village closed the church. All of the believers then used to come to pray in front of the closed church.

One day, without consulting the people, the local authorities came accompanied by several militiamen with dogs and they surrounded the church and then some young men blew up the church in a barbaric way. They destroyed all the archives of our ancient culture. This happened in the 'period of stagnation'. People asked to make a museum out of the ruins of the church, but no one would listen to them. The chairman of our collective farm was later punished for the destruction, because the church turned out to be a rather ancient and valuable historical monument.

Our people have to go to pray in neighbouring villages. I am rather old now, eighty-eight years, and I am disabled from the war so I can't walk long distances. So I built a small chapel in my yard and I wanted to move it to a place close by but the local authorities would not give me permission. I have asked everyone I can in the district but instead of any help or assistance I was threatened with fines if I moved the chapel. They tell me that they will even come to my yard and destroy this chapel.

I, together with the people of my village, fought for this land against our enemies. I didn't grudge my blood for that. Haven't I deserved a small piece of land for all that? I am very old and not much is left for me in this world. But let my chapel remain. Let other believers and me pray for the consolidation of peace throughout the world so that our generation and our children will never again suffer or witness such terrible wars.

V. Simachuk, Ilnitza, Western Ukraine.

70

I don't think we should teach divinity at school. But I support the idea of publishing the Bible and the Gospel. It's strange why these books are banned in this country and are considered to be anti-Soviet literature. I have read the Gospel published before the Revolution. Most of the ideas expressed in the Gospel remain true now and will continue to be so in the years to come. There are many apophthegms wrongfully thought of as belonging to our authorities. Maybe that is the reason why they don't want the Bible or the Gospel to be published?

In short, I suggest that we should have lessons on morality and spirituality at school. The pupils should study the Bible and the main religions. It will help us to raise the morality of our young people.

Rostov, medical, worker, City of Chelyabinsk.
Pansilev, City of Gorky.

IT's painful to realize that so many relics of the past have disappeared in our country. The Press is full of pictures of relics which were destroyed during the Stalin regime, the Khrushchev regime and the Brezhnev regime – for instance the Serpikov Kremlin, the Sukarev tower, monuments to Russian princes and emperors and the warriors of Russia. It was through the ignorance and vandalism of the Soviet leaders that the monuments to Alexander the Second, General Skobalev and many other outstanding people of Russia were destroyed.

As a rule, these monuments were of great artistic value. It was announced that everything was being done in the name of the people, who approved of this kind of activity wholeheartedly. On the other hand any leader while he was still alive tried to immortalize himself and during his lifetime many monuments were erected. Well, the leadership has changed, perestroika has begun and now there are hotheads who suggest that the monuments erected during the Stalin regime should be destroyed. Unfortunately, history repeats itself. Some people even demand that Stalin's accomplices buried in the Kremlin wall should be removed.

Now many laws are passed. Perhaps they should pass a law to preserve everything connected with history, no matter whether we approve of it or not.

Nikolsky.

ALEXEI Grigorievich Stakhanov [*the legendary coal miner who distinguished himself with record quotas in 1935 and whose surname became a figure of speech for superhuman dedication*] was someone whose ascent to glory was greeted with applause from some people and with mistrust and scepticism from others.

That Alexei Stakhanov was able to hew 102 tons of coal with his miners is beyond doubt. But the famous fourteen-ton daily quotas cannot be regarded as true. A face worker, apart from hewing his coal, is also supposed to secure the pit face. The quota depends on the geological conditions and varies between five to ten tons per shift. It was the same in the 1930s.

During his record-breaking shift Stakhanov was helped by two experienced workers (Borisenko and Shchigolev) who secured the pit face for him. Therefore the 102 tons should be divided between the three of them which means that each man turned in five daily quotas, a record in itself.

People who reported the record to the authorities obviously wanted to make the figure even more impressive than it actually was.

Shchigolev and Borisenko were never mentioned at all when the party branch of the Tsentralnaya-Irmino mine published the results of the record-breaking shift on 31 August 1935. This inaccuracy led to subsequent debates and misunderstandings.

After Stakhanov set his record on 31 August 1935, many face workers exceeded the 102-ton level. Dokanov, Pozdnyakov, Kontsedalov and Stakhanov himself reached the 200-ton mark, while the famous Nikita Izotov brought the record to 640 tons.

There was no talk, however, of anybody achieving twenty to ninety daily quotas during one shift. If the workers who secured the face during the record-breaking shifts were counted, the output of coal per miner would vary between thirty to forty tons per shift. Apparently, this figure sets the limit for hewing coal with a miner's pick. The same is corroborated by contemporary experience.

We met with Stakhanov quite often during a period of ten years or more in both official and informal situations. He always made the point that he had set his record in a team of three.

Does the above belittle the feats of Alexei Stakhanov and other miners? Of course it doesn't! The Stakhanov drive came as a strong factor for higher productivity in the 1930s. The drive deserves respect, and it does not need any exaggerations.

K. Sapitsky, Ph.D. in technology.
S. Lyubovenkov, deputy director, Torezantrasit production group, Donetsk.

AN economically developed country with a backward culture sounds like nonsense. Can a slave create a prosperous society? Yet art can turn a slave into a master. During her most turbulent times, Russia rose to greatness through her exceptional talents – Pushkin, Tchaikovsky, Dostoyevsky. Thank heavens, the memory of these names has remained unsullied.

Nowadays we have the opportunity to promote new talents and original ideas – contemporary as well as those of the past. I am not talking about the creation of a new Eden; what I have in mind is feasible and within reach.

Thousands of volumes of ancient Slavonic literature, historical documents, memoirs, and pre-Revolutionary publications of priceless historical value, are mouldering away in the basement archives of Moscow, and not only Moscow. They must be dug out of the recesses of oblivion; they desperately need the light of day.

In the depths of music archives, unique records of ancient Slavonic musical culture are hidden. Unfortunately, we do not have the technical skills and equipment to decode these strange musical scores. Private collections hold works of art which would be the pride and joy of any State museum. But there will be no private exhibitions nor bequests if we do not learn to treat art and the private collector with due respect. Legislation is needed which would explain to the nation the link between economic growth and the resources needed to promote the development of art forms. Such a law should provide for trustees, i.e. a government institution, which would not deal with culture in general, but which would become the RSFSR's [Russia's] administrative centre for art. The trustee institution would be responsible for setting up, running and co-ordinating cultural centres, conventions, associations and other activities, thus sparing the artists a great deal of time and trouble, and the State. Consequently, it would be sensible to set up special art commissions in all local, regional and provincial councils, as well as the Supreme Soviet. An art trustee centre could then operate through such administrative bodies in all Russian towns and allocate funds in close accordance with artists' requirements. It would become the artists' trustee. All professional artists (and I do mean 'professional', not 'commercial') must be aware that there is a certain risk involved. Non-professional artists and all types of handicraft would remain under the Ministry of Culture.

Hopefully we shall find art patrons who would be prepared to consider my suggestions. In any case, there is always room to discuss it. A tidal wave of freedom is sweeping through the RSFSR Supreme Soviet and the Moscow Soviet of People's Deputies, giving us hope that Russian art which has miraculously survived the bad times will at long last be given the attention that it deserves.

A. Makhlin, student, All-Union Institute of
Cinematographic Art.

RECENTLY the announcer on the TV programme *600 Seconds* [*a Leningrad TV current affairs programme also receivable in Moscow*] told the viewers that in Leningrad an initiative group had been formed striving for the restoration of the former name of the city. In the opinion of the organizers there were no grounds for the renaming of Petrograd.

Of course we know a lot of examples of Soviet people going to bed in one city and waking up in another. Such was the case with the citizens of Tver, Samara and many others. That's why the demands for the restoration of the former names of the cities are justified and they should be supported by Soviet public opinion. In this connection I should like to remind the members of the initiative group and their supporters that the city was named in honour of Lenin at the request of the Petrograd proletariat and the idea was supported by all the working people of the Soviet Union. In this respect Leningrad is an exception because it got its name at the will of all of the Soviet people.

It should be noted that many people wrongfully think that before 1924 Petrograd bore the name of its founder, Peter the Great. This is historically wrong. The city was named Petersburg in honour of St Peter so the question arises, why should the city get back its former name, the name of a Christian saint?

It should be added that we have no right to revise the decision of a whole generation of Soviet people, contemporaries of Great October, to immortalize the memory of the leader of the proletarian revolution.

Korstelov, Moscow region.

(There is pressure in cities throughout the Soviet Union which were renamed after the Revolution or through the years of Stalin to revert to their 'pre-Revolutionary' identities – Ed.)

Question and Answer

I would like to know how many different peoples and nationalities there are within the Soviet Union today. The Press gives widely differing figures.

K. Sirotkin, Novgorod.

E. Tenishev, Associate Member of the USSR Academy of Sciences, Head of Laboratory of Turkology and Mongolistics, USSR Academy of Sciences Institute of Linguistic Studies, answers:

The national population census of 1926 gives about 200 different nations. During Stalin's time the official list of nations within the USSR fell to sixty, and since 1977 the USSR Central Statistics Directorate has claimed 101.

The list of peoples and language of the USSR, which was used in the recent national census, includes 128 'nationalities'. By joint agreement with the USSR Academy of Sciences' Ethnographic Institute another forty peoples were recently added to this. But these statistics are not the final story, of course. Not long ago we received a list from a

Byelorussian enthusiast in Minsk, Mr A. F. Klimchuk, containing approximately 400 different peoples within the USSR. It is possible that once this list has been studied in depth we may be adding even more to the final total.

HOW many towns had the name of Stalin?

C. Mamedev, Baku.

A. Fishman answers:
The 'great leader' gave this 'great honour' to six towns (without taking into account numerous villages). In July 1924 the important town of Donbas was renamed Stalino. Its previous name was Yusefka (or Useva). The previous name was connected with the metal-making plant which was built there in 1869 by a Welshman, John Hughes. Then in April 1925 the town of Tsaritsin was renamed Stalingrad. In October 1929, on the eve of the reformation of Tajikistan from autonomy into the southern republic, its capital Duchambe became Stalinabad. In 1932 the town of Kusnetz, glorified by V. Mayakovsky (Novakusnetz), was turned into Stalinsk.

Stalin wanted to put his name even higher than Lenin. Later in 1934 two more were added. Staliniri (Tsinvalli in Georgia) and Stalinagorsk (formerly Bobriki) in the limits of the Moscow Region of those days. After the twenty-second council of the CPSU in 1961, when much was spoken about the cult of personality and Stalin and mass repression, all these titles disappeared from the map of our Motherland. Novakusnetz and Tsinvalli were given back their former names. The capital of the Tajik republic was renamed Duchambe. The other three towns were given new names. Stalingrad became Volgograd, Stalino, Danietsk; Stalinagorsk, Novamoscov (Tula region).

Only now in Albania is the name continued.

ACCORDING to the Ministry of Communication there has been a 150 per cent increase in the amount of correspondence lost or misappropriated in the USSR over the past year. How much longer must we put up with this?

L. Pfaifer, Kustanay.

According to the Ministry of Communications of the USSR, misappropriation of internal and foreign correspondence in the first half of 1989 was valued at R531,000, of which R478,000 was estimated to be the fault of the Post Office. There has also been a marked increase in complaints that foreign mail does not reach its destination in the Soviet Union. Complaints come especially from citizens with friends or relatives in the USA, Canada, West Germany and Australia. Letters, parcels and hard currency postal orders regularly disappear. Rumours that a gang of criminals had entrenched itself in the Moscow General Post Office in order to steal money and souvenirs from foreign mail were discounted – *AIF*.

CHAPTER THREE

ENVIRONMENT AND HEALTH

Chernobyl and its consequences have dramatically focused atten-
tion on environmental and health issues in the Soviet Union.
Soviet industry is 'dirtier' than in the West and spends less on
clean-ups. The USSR also spends less on health care than the USA
– 4.5 per cent of its GDP compared to 10 per cent. The annual
health expenditure per person is just eighty roubles compared to
1,772 in the USA. Not surprisingly, the Soviet citizen can expect
to die five years before his or her American counterpart (at
seventy) and to be far less healthy in life. Infant mortality is 24.7
per 1,000 live births, against ten in the USA; 47.7 mothers per
100,000 die in childbirth, compared to eight in the USA. And a
Soviet person is around five times more likely to contract TB,
sixty times more likely to catch measles – whooping cough is
more than seven times as prevalent. The good news is that the rate
of syphilis and gonorrhoea appears to be less than half that of the
USA, although, as some of the following letters explain, doubt
should be cast on the official figures.

Infant mortality is one of the most important medical-
demographic indicators of a nation's health and the USSR's rate,
approaching that of some developing countries – up to five times
worse than many Western countries – masks some even more
unpalatable facts. Some of the Central Asian republics have death
rates of up to fifty-three per thousand and investigations by
government agencies there have shown that around 86 per cent of

infant deaths are not even registered (60 per cent in Moldavia, 50 per cent in Russia).

Schoolchildren are also unhealthy. The head of the State Committee for Education said recently that only a quarter of schoolchildren could be considered to be completely healthy; up to 30 per cent of primary school children have speech problems, 15–20 per cent suffer from nervous or psychological disorders, and more than 50 per cent of pre-school children have some kind of health problem. He went on to say that the standard of health does not improve during the years of education: 45 per cent of those leaving school have chronic disorders and every fifth student in higher education is in need of medical care. More than a million mothers every day are unable to work because their children are ill and every year the country loses nine billion roubles through sickness of workers or mothers with sick children.

CHERNOBYL AND NUCLEAR ISSUES

MY sister's family (herself, her husband and their three children) was one of the resettled families following the Chernobyl disaster. In 1986 they were evacuated from the village of Novoe Sharko (Narodich region, Zhitomir province) and brought to live in Narodich, eight kilometres away from their old village. They've been living there for four years now, they've had gas and telephone lines installed, they've been paid compensation. A great deal of money was spent on the whole resettlement project. Yet, in the area where they live now, radiation is still twenty to thirty times above the permitted level. People are falling ill all the time: heart and circulatory problems, anaemia, headaches, leg pains, etc.

Recently they've been promised another resettlement. Where? Literally next door, still in Zhitomir province. A mockery is made of human lives. If all this trouble is taken to resettle people, can't a new village be built some 400–500 km. away from the contaminated area? The cost will be the same. All that people want is the certainty that they are no longer living in a danger zone.

Clearly our wealthy State can afford costly resettlement projects every three to four years. Why couldn't people from the disaster zone be moved to safe areas once and for all? Millions of roubles could have been saved. I feel desperately sorry for my sister (she is only thirty-one) and her family. What does the future hold in store for them?

What terrible effects will a long-term exposure to radiation have upon their health?

A. Stronavana, Tula.

I was born and grew up in Beskaragai village, Seliyarsk, situated some 200 km. from Semipalatinsk towards the nuclear testing zone. I remember the 'exercises' very well. There was no school on those days. Now, nuclear testing is carried out underground, but in those days it was done in the open.

On those days, we were herded into a deep ravine and told to lie on the ground, face down, with the mouth wide open (the latter was supposed to protect our eardrums from bursting). But of course we children wanted to see what was happening. So we watched. We saw three nuclear bomb carriers circle the sky, drop the bomb, and promptly fly away. The bomb would be slowly descending, in the glow of a blinding white light. When it fell, a cloud would rise up in the air, assuming the characteristic mushroom shape. The mushroom cloud was whitish- or greyish-pink, and it billowed and whirled and grew across the sky, eventually breaking into smaller clouds, before falling upon the earth, upon the fields and the River Irtysh. It all depended on the wind.

Sometimes, it would blow towards Abolsk region, at other times towards us. There was also the sound wave. It would come more or less immediately, knocking people off their feet. Cats, dogs, cattle and other domestic animals would run away in panic, meowing, barking and lowing, adding to the noise of whining sirens. It was terrible, like the end of the world.

Our school was the only two-storey building in our village. During one of the exercises, the top storey was sliced off, like with a knife. Many houses collapsed. Later, soldiers built a new school for us, and rebuilt the houses. After tests carried out in winter, the weather would change and it would be warm, like summer, with the ice on the River Irtysh melting completely. Sometimes the tests would be carried out at night-time. Children were woken up and dragged out of bed in haste, dressed warmly, if it was winter, and taken to the ravine. At night, the effect was truly spectacular: it was brighter than full sunshine; one could have picked needles out of a haystack.

I have so many memories from those days, it would take too much time to tell them all. We used to hear a lot about Hiroshima and Nagasaki and weren't Americans awful, testing their nuclear weapons on humans. Yet no one ever mentioned that in the Soviet Union nuclear bombs were being tested on humans, i.e. on us. Clearly, we were not considered humans then – or now, for that matter. There were never any medical check-ups, in spite of the radiation we were exposed to. People in our village began to die of leukaemia, but for some reason it had to be kept quiet, and we children knew nothing about the mysterious illness. In 1963 my family moved to Urdshar, a village still in the same province, but 560 km, south of Semipalatinsk.

I was a student in a technical school, my brother was also at school in Semipalatinsk, the others had left home by then. Afterwards I worked for two years in town and then went back to Urdshar where I stayed till 1986. My parents died, father at fifty-seven, mother at fifty-nine. On 2 January 1986, I gathered my family and we left for Novokuznetsk, where my other relatives live. They had written to us, telling us that the food situation in Novokuznetsk was not too bad. In our province, there was hardly anything to eat. Until 1989 we didn't know that Novokuznetsk was the environmentally cleanest town in the Soviet Union.

I would like to know why we, who have endured years of nuclear testing and its grim effects, were never given any compensation. People who work in conditions hazardous to health are allowed to retire early, yet we who have lived in an area where everything you touched was a health hazard are given absolutely nothing. I am forty-eight and constantly ill. I have high blood pressure, heart ischaemia and a number of other disorders. It's not that I want to complain, I simply want to know whether we who survived nuclear testing can expect any help now. There were never any benefits for us, no sanatoria when we needed them, no special funds – nothing.

L. Boikova, builder.

RECENTLY there was a meeting between members of the government commission dealing with the after-effects of the Chernobyl disaster and members of the Byelorussian community. And, according to radio and TV and newspaper articles, everything is now known. The media gave detailed information about the health of people in the affected areas, information about agriculture and provided maps of 'dirty' territories. However, there are still many questions to be answered. Here, we want to know not just about regions but specific information about every village. Inaccurate information only fuels speculation. When people here feel even the slightest bit ill they consider it to be connected to Chernobyl after-effects. And I think there are grounds for this alarm.

Some of the villages of our region border the uninhabited zones. Only the River Pripit is between us. Our meadows and fields for cows and other land of our collective farm runs up to the river. Another portion of our land is near to the town of Narovly which is considered to be unsafe. From time to time our regional newspaper gives summaries of the radiation conditions in our region, but the articles are foggy. Besides, we are told not to use the milk from our cows, not to pick berries and mushrooms from our forest, not to eat vegetables from our kitchen gardens without testing them and not to fish.

So, how can we test vegetables if we have no special instruments? It would be easier to deal with the fear of radiation if we could actually see it. People should be equipped with geiger counters. This lack of information leads to sad, grievous consequences.

Many people now don't work in their gardens. We are also trying to sell all our cows, hens and geese. Before the disaster, in our village of Barbaro there were more than 120 cows. Now there are only thirty-four. In our region, where there are eight villages, only eighty-one cows remain of 400. So now, of course, we have to shop in the towns for our food. A lot of time has passed since Chernobyl and we should be given full information about all the possible after-effects we could experience. We want to live a normal life, not one of adapting to our worst fears. But for that we need every last detail of information, no matter how unpalatable.

E. Ignatovich, Gomel region.

MY mother, who lives in the Bryansk region, suffered as a result of the Chernobyl catastrophe and has been receiving thirty roubles a month as some kind of compensation. Some people call this 'coffin money'. This winter the payment was increased to fifty-five roubles. My mother gets this money personally. None of her relatives can get it for her, even if they have her authorization. And it is not possible to pay the money directly into the bank either. So, if my mother comes to visit me or decides to have a rest in a nursing home, she loses the money.

I want to know who set up such an inhuman and humiliating order? You are given with one hand and it is taken away with the other. Is it the fault of our local authorities or are the orders given from the centre?

R. Chestakova, Saransk.

WE are from Narovly which suffered as a result of the Chernobyl catastrophe. The point is that we have to be moved to another place – maybe in 1991 or 1992 or in 1995, that's for sure – as it's impossible to live where we are now. But at the same time in the city the construction is still taking place of multi-storeyed buildings and other buildings and projects are under construction, such as an embankment at the House of Pioneers. Tell us please why it is necessary to spend money and construction materials on objects which will not be in use while at the same time we are still living in our houses and have not been moved into a clean zone?

Citizens of Narovly, Gomel region.

THE Chernobyl disaster in 1986 seriously polluted the Khvastovichsky region in Kaluga district where we live. For the first few years the real effects were covered up and the public were told that everything was all right. Now, four years on, we have all begun to notice that we don't feel as good as we used to. Many of us are affected by sleepiness, sickness, dizziness and a lot of people are suffering from heart and artery disease. In 1990 they started paying us all an allowance of R1.15 per family member per month and giving us a certain quota of food products per month. Around here this is known as the 'coffin allowance'.

Summer is coming and soon all the school kids will be on holiday, but what are we going to do with ourselves, since we are not supposed to swim, sunbathe, pick mushrooms or berries or do any of the other things we usually do. Our schools and local leaders are trying to send us to State farms to do agricultural work despite the fact that they know that the ground there is also polluted.

By decree of the Council of Ministers, Bryansk district and others are going to be able to send all their children to holiday camps and centres during the summer vacations. What about us? Aren't we people too?

Schoolchildren of Khvastovichsky region. Age 16.

THERE were rumours in Omsk region about harmful radiation and that the walls of some apartments were the sources of the high level of radiation. The local evening newspaper carried out some kind of investigation and it turned out that in the manufacturing of concrete components for these buildings in the local factory aggregate from Makinskya quarry of Tselinagrat region was used. Something like 92 per cent of the aggregate was from Makinskya and this aggregate with a high level of radiation is supposed only to be used in the construction of roads and industrial buildings. Incidentally, the first classification on different structural materials regarding their radioactivity and the restrictions of their use to particular categories of construction was introduced only in 1976. In Omsk region this classification is ignored. This aggregate should never have been used in the construction of apartment buildings.

When the paper published its investigation a commission was set up for the control of harmful radiation and a meeting of the regional committee took place. After the first tests on gamma background in recently constructed buildings, it was discovered that the centre which carried out these tests falsified them, and adjusted their instruments to show low levels. Four months later the true readings were taken. Tests were carried out on different floors of a building which was under construction. At the ceiling the readings were thirty-eight, on the floor thirty-four X-rays per hour, in the kindergarten bedroom twenty-six and in the musical and sports hall up to thirty – in a swimming pool from thirty-six to thirty-eight.

Apart from that, the by-product of uranium, Rad 226, irradiates the radioactive gas radon which provides an additional dose of radiations. The measurements showed that radiation was three to three and a half times higher than background radiation outside and the iron and concrete parts of buildings normally protect people from this.

There is another rather curious fact. In the building which houses the headquarters of the committee for nature protection the instruments showed a reading of only twelve – that is three times less than in the kindergarten. It proves again that in places where Makinskya aggregate was not used it is lower.

Dozens of letters were received by the evening paper asking for advice about what to do, where to move to. There is no danger to life at the moment from this radiation level but even such a small dose increases the danger of oncological diseases. And the higher the doses the higher is the risk. It is also quite clear that it will not be possible to move all the affected people into safe places. But it is necessary to immediately stop using this aggregate and not increase the number of flats with this high level of radiation.

The regional leadership, however, took a holding position. It is well known that any unjustified radiation of human beings is illegal. In Omsk they prefer not to think about this. And aggregate from Makinskya quarry is still being used to this day.

S. Komarovski, Omsk.

RECENTLY, there has been a lot in the papers and on TV about radioactivity in contaminated areas. I am a specialist in radiation safety and it totally eludes me how the authors can determine the degree of contamination of an area of e.g. one km.^{2} and express it in units of radioactivity (curie) per square kilometre (i.e. Ci/km.^{2}). Our whole team has been pondering over this issue for a long time: how can the radioactivity of an area be estimated on the strength of Ci/km.^{2} data? How can this unit be converted into 'disintegrations'?

As far as I know, the degree of radioactive contamination is measured in the following units: for liquids – disintegrations/min. per cm^3; disintegrations/min. per litre; curie/litre; milicurie/litre; for areas – disintegrations/min. per cm^2. Also, in field conditions, the degree of contamination is estimated by the strength of the dose emitted by the contaminated object (here: soil) of a particular surface area (1–2 cm) in bn/h.

Please judge for yourself: if a specialist who deals with radioactivity every day cannot assess existing radioactive conditions on the strength of these data, can a layman, an ordinary farmer for example, work it out for himself?

Therefore I suggest that the following reports should be regularly published in the Press (with the use of proper units!):

1. Reports based on proper measurements and factual data concerning the degree of radioactive contamination of particular areas. For comparison, permitted radioactive standards should be printed alongside.

2. Reports forecasting any changes in radioactive conditions based on the half-life of the isotopes with the longest period of disintegration which can accumulate in a human body. Also reports on the radioactivity of water reservoirs in contaminated areas.

I. Grigorev, officer, Murmansk.

DEAR People's Deputies, health service workers, twice a year we are forced to be X-rayed. It has been mentioned in the Press that fluorometry is far from being harmless. It is especially bad for women's health. In the West they gave it up long ago because it is barbarous. I have been working in a school for twenty years and I have had fluorometry forty times.

Pigulyevskaya, on behalf of the teachers of school no. 24, Gorky.

I was not upset when the managers of the housing construction combine insisted on putting His Majesty the Plan before all else and put up their highly radioactive pebbledash panels, nor when the health inspectors came along to measure the radiation counts in our apartments and told us that we had thirty microoentgens per hour below the norm, as though Kazakhstan were a special case. But I was upset when I saw Mr Ligachev on a TV programme about the Soviet Children's Fund, when he announced that they had set aside R60 million for children's homes.

This money should be set aside to help sick children who are suffering from the cavalier attitude of adults towards nature, from the consequences of their elders who understand damn all about ecology and care even less. I am talking about children suffering from leukaemia. In the whole of this huge country of ours we still do not have one single specialized children's haematological hospital, and the hospitals that do have special departments are desperately short of cash.

I know what I am talking about because not so long ago I lost my nine-year-old son who was being treated in the haematological department of Moscow's Paediatric Institute. The department is terribly understaffed, with two nurses trying to do everything, but not managing half of it. There are a lot of seriously ill children there, they need painkilling injections for which they have to wait an hour or more. There are not enough ancillary staff, so the parents of sick children are to be found helping to wash floors and corridors in an area of the hospital which should in theory be super clean.

The doctors and specialists there are good and know what they are doing, but with the parlous state of the hospital's finances, they are banging their heads against a brick wall trying to give the children the treatment they should be having.

When the parents of children suffering from leukaemia asked the Soviet Children's Fund for help, they were turned down and told to find sponsors elsewhere. If the Soviet Children's Fund, a charitable public organization, is not able to recognize a priority when it sees one, then we are not left with much hope for the future. It is better to cure a dozen bright little children suffering from leukaemia than it is to artificially prolong the lives of mentally retarded children, whose lives will not be made any the more joyous for this help.

S. Zhusanbaev, deputy head of Mathematics Department,
Tselinograd Engineering and Construction Institute.

MY town, Baranovichi, which is a small provincial centre, relies on charity as much as other Soviet localities. Our local paper, *The Communist Banner*, frequently publishes appeals to the public on behalf of the less fortunate. Here is one of the most recent stories:

Inna Sanyut, twelve-year-old daughter of a local railwayman, fell ill and was diagnosed as suffering from acute leukaemia, caused by exposure to radiation. After a three-year treatment in the First Minsk Clinic, the doctors came to the cheerless conclusion that further treatment was pointless unless a bone marrow transplant could be performed. Their advice was to take the child to a cancer clinic abroad, thus admitting their failure. Everyone knows how expensive such operations are; no less than R100,000 in foreign currency.

In vain did the father of the unfortunate girl appeal repeatedly to the Soviet Children's Fund, famous for its charity marathons in similar cases, and to the USSR Ministry of Health.

The position is not only tragic; it is additionally complicated by the fact that a hundred similar cases, i.e. children with acute leukaemia, are waiting for treatment in Baranovichi Children's Hospital, as was officially confirmed by the hospital's chief consultant, V. M. Zenevich. The trouble is that the official bodies usually make one or two ineffective appeals through one or two of their people, resulting in a brief bout of publicity which, in the long run, does not bring any real help. Such single spurts of charity, for all the commotion they make, convey in the end one message: there is no money to save one sick child, let alone any others, so grin and bear it or do the best you can by yourself.

And so people suffer in silence, putting their faith in long-term ecological programmes, not realizing that all around them massive financial resources are being used to purchase goods abroad which have nothing whatsoever to do with saving the lives of dying children.

I have found a number of very interesting facts in *Seven Days*, Byelorussia's official weekly information guide. Here are some figures, published on 29 April, concerning the use of foreign currency resources by certain institutions and enterprises. In view of the present economic situation in the Soviet Union, these facts and figures undoubtedly have a certain poignancy. For example: during the past year, the

Management of the Automobile Inspection Department of the USSR Ministry of Internal Affairs bought thirty-four cars in the USA, Germany and Japan, including a Mercedes for the director. In Gomel province (one of the places hardest hit by the nuclear disaster), Lesokhimkombinat Association and Stroiavtomatika Factory bought their directors a Ford each; Kristall Factory and Mozyr Cable Factory, a Nissan each; Myasomolprom Industrial Association – a Toyota. In Bobruisk, the directors of several local factories (textiles, leather, and down-and-feather products in Berezov region), all drive brand-new Fords. 'Belvest' boasts two Mercedes limousines and a Volkswagen; Vitebsk Television Factory – two Nissans; Novopolock Neftetargsintez Industrial Association – three Toyotas and the Domestic Control Office – one Toyota.

So you see, dear *Argumenty i Fakty*, there is an acute shortage of foreign currency for some, yet others will continue to exchange their firms' Volgas for the more prestigious Western limousines.

I know what they would say: the money comes from different coffers. That is why we need new deputies, i.e. people who can work out new economic mechanisms and new tax policies, so that the necessary funds can be obtained at a moment's notice in order to save a child's life.

M. Kurei, Baranovichi, Brest province.

INADEQUACIES, PROBLEMS AND SOLUTIONS

THESE days, a suitable slogan for the work of children's dental surgeons could well be 'All the worst for our children!' There are no drill heads. And this is not a passing shortage, but a continuous lack of them. The life of a single head is six months. Our specialized dental clinic which employs fifteen dental surgeons gets two drill heads per year. Can you imagine a dentist trying to drill a child's tooth using a broken drill head?

It is common for a dentist to fish inside a child's mouth in search of a drill tip which has detached itself from the damaged head. Also, drill tips swivel in a worn head and can seriously damage the inside of the child's mouth. There is a shortage of drill tips, too. We have to use old, blunt tips, sawing decayed teeth like pieces of timber. An adult would not stand such torment, let alone a child.

In our dental clinic, we have old-type bur drills, whereas adult clinics have the most advanced new equipment. Filling material is of a poor quality and there is not enough of it. How can a young child withstand such treatment? No wonder that children are so frightened of us and have to be dragged to the dentist, screaming. We are their tormentors. Yet tooth decay can be the source of many other disorders that affect not only the mouth, but the whole of the human organism.

The government's attitude to health care is a true indication of its attitude to the nation. Everyone knows how the government treats health care . . . No need to say more.

Employees of Polyclinic no. 3 [*seventeen signatures in all*],
Kuibyshev.

HOW can we get money to cure the sick? The principle of our medicine seems to be that the more beds we can provide the more people we can cure. But beds don't cure people, doctors and medicine do. An enterprise can buy expensive and not always necessary equipment but if a worker falls ill the enterprise cannot give money for his treatment although many clever leaders say that we should do it. We have estimated that if doctors could receive R300–350 per operation then our surgery could become self-financing and we could do many more operations than now.

But for all this it's necessary to change existing practice. I propose as an experiment that bills for operations should be given to the enterprises whose employees and members of their families use the clinics.

A. Muldashov, Leader of All-Russia Centre of Plastic Surgery,
Novokuznetsk.

MOTHERS of dying children are writing this letter to you from Novosibirsk. Our children are seriously ill with blood cancer but they are getting virtually no treatment in the haematology department of the children's clinic No. 8. The treatment takes place under horrible conditions. There are eight seriously ill patients in each room, not including the mothers of the children. Children are dying in front of other children. There is a shortage of drugs to undertake proper courses of treatment as sometimes the hospital doesn't receive drugs for months on end. That's why children are dying and their parents are suffering. And across the road there is another hospital, No. 16, for the 'merited' people of the city, where in one room there is only one – or at most two – patients. And the toilets there are not at the end of the corridor. All the requests and demands of mothers to the authorities have gone unanswered. You must understand the despair we are in. Our children need to have normal procurements of drugs and new methods of treatment. Most of their short lives are spent in a dark and gloomy hospital. Couldn't the building of a new clinic be speeded up and greater initiative given to the development of new methods and their application? Our children cannot wait. It is going to be too late for them.

Thirty-one signatures, no. 8 Children's Clinic, Novosibirsk.

RECENTLY I read an article on insurance in *Argumenty i Fakty*, no. 20. It was called 'Who Benefits From Insurance?'

and was about the draft law on insurance prepared by the management of the USSR State Insurance. Several points clearly indicate that, from now on, insurance policies will leave the customer much worse off than before. Here is an example: Following a highly publicized massive outbreak of food poisoning in a factory belonging to the Ufa Industrial Association, employees who had taken out insurance against personal accidents quite rightly applied to State Insurance for compensation, for medical expenses and physical suffering which, in a case of severe food poisoning, were considerable. However, Bakshir ASSR Council of Ministers confirmed in the resolution of 28 April 1990 passed by its Extraordinary Committee that the outbreak was caused by contaminated food, prepared and served in the factory canteen, in-plant, with a total disregard for food hygiene and sanitary regulations, and with no proper supervision.

I would like to see a food inspector who manages to sneak to the kitchens of a regimented enterprise and carries out his inspection without prior notice!

How did State Insurance respond to the workers' appeal? Every single application was categorically turned down. It turns out that compensation is granted in cases of '. . . accidental and acute food poisoning with the exception of toxic infections'. Any doctor can tell you that the medical term for food poisoning is 'toxic food infection' and this is what he has to write as his official diagnosis.

Consequently, what State Insurance writes is, in fact, 'cases of food poisoning except cases of food poisoning'.

It is clear now that this confusion has been cunningly devised by the management of the USSR State Insurance and laid out, rule by rule, in its booklet (see section no. 49 on Insurance Against Personal Accidents), so that no insured person is entitled to even the smallest compensation in the aforementioned cases. Are the authors of the brochure genuinely ignorant of the official terminology? Who benefits from State Insurance? The State, it appears. The State, which feeds us contaminated food and then fleeces us by tricking us into paying phoney insurance premiums that will give us no compensation for expense and suffering.

M. Elagina, Ufa.

ANNUAL expenses on the maintenance of the State Security Department seem a miserly sum when compared with the enormous losses suffered by the economy, the environment and people's health, due to unwarranted secrecy. State Security withholds important information from appropriate Soviet bodies in the sphere of architecture, the use of land, health care and environmental protection.

I shall explain, using my own region as an example. Recently, land improvement specialists reclaimed 1,000 hectares (2,470 acres) of land for growing fodder crops to be used by a local State farm and a battery farm. However, it soon turned out that half of the drained land belonged to a specially designed water protection zone around reservoirs which supply the local town (regional centre) with water. According to current environmental planning and building regulations, no mineral or organic fertilizers may be used in the water protection zone.

A similar zone is planned near Archangel. Many towns and villages will be affected by water protection regulations. The introduction of water protection zones will involve the closure or a change of location for many factories, buildings, cemeteries, etc. Many people will have to move. The present law forbids mining of minerals in the vicinity of water reservoirs and in water protection zones. The trouble is, if people do not know where the zones are, or are going to be, how can they be expected to comply with this law?

Every region in the Soviet Union has experienced similar problems. The enormous losses are not only of a financial or material nature. People are beginning to lose hope for a better future.

A sensible revision of the confidential information register would benefit the whole country. Every region and village council should be issued with detailed maps of the area with all its relevant features, such as mineral deposits, sanitary protection zones, protected woodlands, green belts, nature reserves, etc., including plans of future alterations to the environment in connection with planned mining operations.

Such detailed maps would be a great help to many construction and design institutes and building companies. Their surveyors may not have the expertise and the equipment of the official surveying bodies and they often put in a great deal of time and effort into investigating areas which have already been properly surveyed – only there is no access to the data.

A. Pleshkov, specialist in the use of land, Archangel province.

I often read about the elimination of privilege and the turning over of special rest homes and clinics for the élite to the people and the State. Honestly, I can't believe any of this because I'm working myself in one of these places. It is called Titskova and it is designed for 400 people altogether. But this rest home is normally functioning for two to three months a year and during this time only about 200 people or a little more have rest. The rest of the time – eight or nine months – this place is practically empty, with only thirty to fifty. But what a palace it is. It's an enormous multi-storey building with luxurious rooms. There are also suites but those are for VIPs. The rooms are comfortable with some very expensive things in them about which the common people cannot even dream. There are also two canteens and dachas for rest. All of these premises are empty for eight to nine months a year.

There are so many really ill people, old people, children, those who came back from Afghanistan, disabled people who could have good treatment and health rehabilitation in this place. I have a sick child myself and I was often with him in the district hospital. I know under what horrible conditions our children are given treatment. These hospitals are poor, shabby buildings, providing bad meals and insanitary conditions. You could hardly survive on the food. Just soups and porridges prepared with water. Vegetables, fruit, juices – all these are limited. And sometimes looking at such meals puts you off eating them.

There is a big shortage of the necessary medicines but for the children of the élite the menu and the choice is bigger and better. There is a wide choice of dishes just like in the Western countries – they have salami, good fish, sausages, rare vegetables and fruit. Could it be that the authorities responsible do not know all of this? Could it be that the Ministry of Health does not know? They know, but it is likely that this situation is amenable to them. With respect.

N. S., Kalininska region.

THERE is only one children's clinic in Moscow which is run on the self-accounting system, in a city where there are nine million people. We have highly qualified specialists in it with scientific degrees. In deference to co-operatives, consultations with our specialists can be had by anybody. For instance, one visit to a doctor costs fifty kopecks, a professor's consultation R3.50.

For sixty-three years of its existence conditions in the clinic have barely changed. It was designed for visits of eighty-six people a day but today the clinic deals with 550 children a day. For the last ten years the administration has been fighting for improvements in working conditions but until now all the decisions of the MosSoviet (Moscow Municipality) remain only on paper. Two years ago the decision was taken to construct a new building but to this day there is no land for it. In the centre of Moscow there are some empty apartment buildings but the district executive won't agree to give any of them to the clinic. It could be that it is more profitable to turn over such premises to Intourist hotels than to sick children.

Through television, we addressed the leaders of the district and we got a letter from them in which the deputy chairman, O. Volkov, says that we underestimate the role of the paid servants in the improvement of the living standards of the people and he also criticizes us for refusing to raise our charges by 15 per cent in accordance with the decree of the Council of Ministers.

If there were sufficient premises for the clinic it would be possible to help children from other cities, 80,000 of whom come each year to the Ministry of Health for help. It would also be possible to have more beds for Muscovites and if there were space enough for the medical facilities we could implement the new methods of diagnostics, thus rendering a service to the city, as there are highly qualified specialists working in our clinic.

A. Bescrovnya, Chief Doctor, R. Gritsuk, Secretary, party bureau.

I am writing this letter from hospital. In the last three years the number of diabetic patients has increased by 20 per cent. And the medicine insulin which gives us life, according to the

State committee on statistics of the Russian Federation, reduced by 60 per cent. I don't see any special products or foodstuffs produced and sales girls in shops say they don't receive such products. I think that from a technical point of view, it isn't difficult to start their production.

V. Milishenko, Moscow

WE have a desperate lack of foreign currency for medical equipment, computers and consumer goods. On a recent TV programme an anonymous government minister was quoted as saying that he was ready to find a million dollars so that the first Soviet journalist was launched into space, rather than a Japanese one. This, he said, was for the prestige of the country. Why not usefully spend this money on something like facilities for ultrasonic diagnoses to raise the prestige of our medicine instead? Let us consider what is the real prestige of the country and how we order our priorities.

G. Sergeva, Moscow.

I propose to People's Deputies a number of measures to improve the health system. I believe that if these were adopted it would decisively improve matters in the current year without any additional financial expense.

First. Doctors should be freed from all kinds of reports. They should write in patients files only the diagnosis and the details necessary for certificates for work. It would help to save at a minimum 30 per cent of the working time of the doctors which would be equal to providing 300,000 extra doctors and several thousand medical workers who process such reports.

Second. To evaluate the work of any doctor by final results, criteria to be worked out by the Ministry of Health.

Third. Using the recommendation given by the World Health Organization in 1987 to reduce the expense on X-rays by at least two to three times. That wouldn't decrease the quality of treatment and diagnostics but it would considerably reduce the X-ray loading on the population and the means gained – that's about 5 per cent of the total health budget – could be used for urgent medical needs.

Fourth. To change the order of leave for women before the birth of a child: in total, and together with post-natal leave, it amounts to 112 days. No matter when the child is actually born a gynaecologist must give leave exactly fifty-six days before the estimated birth. But, of course, it's practically impossible to accurately predict the date and this means that women who give birth later than the estimated delivery date get shorter post-natal leave and this can bring physical harm to the woman.

Fifth. We should give up the principle of preventive medicine as modern medicine is of an aggressive character. I'll give only one example. At the All-Union Congress of Doctors in 1988 there was a considerable increase in lung cancer witnessed. In part this could be due to the mass fluorometric testing and the fondness of doctors for using X-rays as a diagnostic technique. (By the way, there are less harmful ways to diagnose TB.) This would result in the still higher growth of cancer diseases and different kinds of inherited birth defects.

A. Alfurev, candidate of medicine.

AIDS AND SEXUAL DISEASES

IT is quite evident that the organization, prevention, treatment and the liquidation of the consequences of Aids in the forthcoming decade will be among the most important social and economic problems of our State. As a specialist and deputy I am surprised, to put it mildly, at the position taken by the leading organizers of our medical service and scientists on the question of the prevention of Aids. They are convinced that the main thing is to provide the population with syringes for single use and systems for the transfusion of blood. I am absolutely sure that such an approach is quite wrong and it will cause our society great damage.

Let's have a look at the annual needs of single-use syringes. First they said two billion were needed. Then the figure became five billion and now it's already six or seven billion. Supposing we have the necessary quantity of syringes, is there any guarantee that there won't be any cases of infection? I'm quite sure there is no guarantee.

I believe the problem can be solved in the following way: Every Soviet citizen – including babies – should be provided with individual syringes for multiple use and a complete set of needles and medical sterilizers. They should also have droppers and stomatological instruments. This will help to reduce the need for syringes and avoid great expense. The population should know the rules for sterilizing their own instruments and that can be taught easily.

Secondly, it's important, in the shortest possible time, to supply the population with contraceptives, first of all condoms.

Thirdly, we should give up the rigid registration of patients with venereal diseases. Instead, the anonymous method of check-up and treatment would make it possible for additional millions of people to get a medical check-up and treatment.

Palenshinka, People's Deputy of the USSR (head doctor of clinic in City of Habarask).

IN the past few years Aids, which is an incurable disease so far, has been at the centre of attention of world public opinion. Mass media gives information about the growth of the spread of the disease. Aids is called the plague of the twentieth century. But if we analyse the sickness rate year after year we will see that the growth of the number of cases was not so great. In 1984 the number of cases was 13,049 and in 1988 it was 58,000. It is groundless to assert that 30–50 per cent of the virus carriers will develop the disease within the next five years. If it were so the number of cases of Aids eight years after it was discovered would be not 150,000 – as is the case now – but at least 2.5 million people.

There are group risks. They are drug addicts, homosexuals and people who have many sex partners. For the rest of the people the possibility of being infected is decreasing after the checking of blood donors was introduced everywhere. That's why in the near future one can expect not only the stabilization of the sickness rate, but its gradual decrease. If people did not die from numerous other diseases there is no reason to believe that Aids would lead to the death of humanity. All that I said before does not mean of course that it is not necessary to work out effective methods of treatment and prevention of Aids and means of diagnosing it.

Professor Rugeyev, Leningrad.

(There is a sick Soviet joke that Aids, the 'twentieth-century plague', just won't affect either Japan or Russia – the first is in the twenty-first century, the latter still in the nineteenth – Ed.)

AIDS is not asleep. The slow spread of Aids only makes it seem that way. Imported into the USSR by a sailor in 1981, the virus in 1988/89 got to over 100 children in the cities of Elista and Volgagrad. It showed at once what it is capable of. The investigation of the first case of Aids in the USSR revealed a chain of seventeen other cases. In my estimation, if no effective measures are taken against Aids there will be at least 200,000 cases by the beginning of the new century in the USSR.

Most of the virus carriers got infected not at the moment the virus was discovered – that was in 1983 – but later, in the middle of the 1980s. So they will fall ill later, in the early 1990s. Some people think that Aids is not more dangerous for humanity than measles or other infectious diseases but in four years the number of cases increased 4.5 times, while the number of cases of measles and tuberculosis remained relatively stable. There is an effective vaccine against measles and there are medicines against tuberculosis and in most cases it is curable. The high death rate is typical of developing countries where the economy is not highly developed. As for Aids, it dealt a heavy blow upon the United States whose economy and medical service are highly developed.

As is known, there are no vaccines or effective medicines against Aids and they are not expected to appear in the near future. That's why the primary task is to curb the spread of Aids. It's a mistake to believe that there exist risk groups. Experience shows that all people irrespective of their will can become virus carriers and only the degree of risk for different people is different. A woman faithful to her husband can't consider herself belonging to a risk group but a husband might be a virus carrier if he had a love affair with another woman or had a blood transfusion after an accident. Many homosexuals and prostitutes are frightened of the Aids scare and give up their usual way of life because of the danger. Aids will spread rapidly if no effective measures are taken.

Pokrovsky, chairman of the Aids Association.

IN *AIF* you published an interview with the State-run Central Institute for Skin Diseases, which gave quite the wrong impression about the state of affairs in Soviet dermatovenereology. According to your statistics the Soviet Union is far ahead of any other country in this field. However, this is not actually the case. At the last plenary session of the USSR Academy of Medical Sciences' Dermatovenereology Council, the very people who produce those statistics were forced to admit that half of those suffering from gonorrhoea and 10 per cent of those with syphilis do not even figure in official statistics.

The main veneral disease clinics in the Soviet Union were set up as long ago as the thirties. The hard attitudes and forceful methods that were sadly typical of those times certainly do not meet modern-day requirements.

Most people who have contracted venereal diseases try to avoid these dreadful skin and veneral disease clinics and to treat themselves at home, often with disastrous results. This has the double effect of producing unrepresentative statistics in the clinics and of obscuring the sources of the diseases.

Some doctors have come up with the idea of offering confidential check-ups for venereal diseases, contagious skin diseases and Aids. They would also eventually like to see confidential treatment for these. The West has long been treating these cases in out-patient departments.

We think that this would help us to reach those sufferers who have not made use of the traditional clinics. During the past year alone the Moscow City Skin and Venereal Disease Clinic, which introduced a confidential diagnosis service, has registered three times as many syphilis sufferers as one would normally expect in a single clinic. The numbers of patients attending other more traditional clinics in Moscow during that period did not fall.

The second great advantage is that when you are dealing with a patient in confidence they feel safer and are far more likely to tell you who their sexual partners are.

The Moscow City Executive Council's Health Directorate is currently talking to the USSR Ministry of Health about reorganizing the clinic service.

T. Bogdan, Head of Specialized Treatment Department, Central
Health Directorate, Moscow City Executive Council.
V. Tits, Chief Dermatovenereologist, Moscow.

THE DISABLED

I was a participant in the Great Patriotic War. I had four wounds, three of them in the right leg. I also had fractures to my back. I am disabled by the war but I am not considered to be war disabled due to the fact that my wounded leg is not 5 cm. shorter than the other one. The health commission has this instruction and as I don't have this difference between my legs I don't qualify!

A. Stekhalov, Dzerzhinsk, Gorky region.

MANY housing complexes for young people are being built all over the country. But what about the invalids? I suggest we build housing blocks for the invalids so that they could live by themselves without asking anyone for help. They should have a whole district to themselves. The houses should have wide doors, galleries, passages and many other things. Each flat should be equipped with various devices and mechanisms which could help the invalid live like a human being. The complex should have a rehabilitation centre, a gym, shops, a hospital, clubs and workshops. Every invalid should have a chance to work in accordance with his desires and ability.

Saragetika, Limor.

I would love to know when our respected elected representatives are going to get around to discussing the disabled and the humiliating annual round of bureaucrats' offices they have to do to get their disablement cards signed. It seems rather odd that a man with a leg missing should have to have his card signed every year to say that he hasn't grown a new one!

This year it will be fifteen years since I got my group 2 disabled card, but the disabled commission have constantly refused to issue it to me in perpetuity. I cannot go anywhere without my wife's help, and she works during the day. So every year she has to take a week's leave in order to do the rounds of the bureaucrats' offices with me. In my opinion all these disablement rules and regulations are badly out of date. I don't need any commission to tell me that I am not well but that I do not qualify for group 3. But for the sake of this piece of paper my wife and I have to drag round offices where people already know very well who I am and what we want. I am not complaining, I simply want to know when we are going to be accorded our rights.

Mr Barkhatov.

I have decided to turn to you for help. There is so much talk in our country about the need for caring for the disabled, but there is no action. I have spoken to many disabled people only to find out that they resent the kind of lives they are forced to lead.

I have been an invalid since childhood. I am not entitled to any benefits as a disabled person. That my left arm ends at the elbow joint and I have only four fingers on my right hand and that I have no toes on my feet apparently does not count at all. Who is there to understand how much trouble it is for me to do the washing, cleaning and cooking, and how difficult it is to walk and that my stump hurts after I have done my washing and my right hand trembles because it is weak? Who is there to help me? No one!

Moreover, there are people who go out of their way to say nasty things to me. Just imagine: ever since I was a child I have always hated how people look at me and sigh. I have to go through humiliation when I talk to the drunken foreman at the artificial limbs plant so that he will make my appliance on time. The appliance is heavy and it hurts when I wear it, but I have to use it so that people will not stare at me. And I have no choice but to put up with the fact that I feel like a real invalid when I wear that limb.

G. Prodma, Chui, Chuisky district.

I read in *AIF* about the benefits and privileges given to Afghan veterans. I want to ask simply, isn't the cost of a man too cheap? Because only those who came back wounded or disabled or received decorations in Afghanistan received these benefits. I don't want to say that people like me who came back uninjured should be on the same level as the wounded. Of course they deserve more attention from the people and the State but, as to the rewards given, I don't think we should divide people who were there into first and second class.

I didn't see many soldiers there receive medals, I only saw their portraits, posthumous, in army headquarters. It could be that many were given medals, but how many were soldiers? When I went to Afghanistan, believe me, the last thing I thought about was benefits or privileges which I could use, or about money or rewards. You can't balance such things against your life or your health. But having been in Afghanistan and having learned that no one needs you with all your problems you have to pity people for their lack of understanding.

It became worse when I read recently that a military ski team and the pilots who flew them were awarded decorations. But there were so many boys who participated in this war, who gave their lives under an Afghanistan sky, and they weren't rewarded or given medals.

My acquaintances who served in Cuba where there is peace and where our people are not killed received many benefits. They got a car without standing in a queue and a lot of other things. And those who were in Afghanistan got nothing. I have been a party member for three years, a young communist, aged twenty-eight, and my views have changed greatly in that time. I do not believe now that everything that is done by the leadership is for the welfare of the people. Does any of them think of the actual price the people have to pay to implement what is decided by them, either on our land or in Afghanistan?

Now I see that there are some rather safe spheres of activity where the fruits of your labour are more vivid. You can buy jeans for R100, you boil them and then you can sell them for R200. And when you have money you can solve your problems yourself. When 'you have bread you have a song'. We used to say not long ago 'we will follow our dear leader.' I have bread for the time being but I am not in the mood to sing.

S. Peerishenko, Narisk.

(There is a huge metal statue in Lenin Prospect, Moscow to Yuri Gagarin, the first cosmonaut, who died in a plane crash. But recently the rumour has been going round that, in fact, he only died recently, in an asylum, having been sent there years ago after giving offence to Brezhnev at a dinner. Argumenty i Fakty *asked for an official government comment on the rumour. The response was, 'no comment' – Ed.)*

THERE has been a lot of discussion about the current state of psychiatry. Not long ago this field of medicine touched on our family. This year my son graduated from college and was called up to the army. The original medical commission who examined him designated him as unbalanced and emotionally unstable and sent him for examination at the regional psychiatric hospital. Now, I don't have anything against such examinations, but what I saw visiting my son in the section of this hospital horrified me. First of all, to get permission to go I had to make a telephone call. In the background I could hear the sound of heavy metal doors clanging. When I went there I went in through such a door and a metal grille was closed behind me. Then I went into the visiting room. To call anybody into this room an inside door was unlocked, behind which I saw an almost indescribable scene. There were more than sixty people, all of whom had been sent for examination by the military commission. They were lying on metal beds without mattresses and as there weren't enough beds for all of them, some were sleeping on the floor. There was only one tiny window and only by opening this could they get ventilation. It was noticeable that all the windows had grilles on them and all the medical workers had keys in their hands and they were constantly locking and unlocking doors.

All of those held are in closed rooms. Some of them are allowed to go to the visiting room where there are tanks of water. If they came in the doctors immediately locked the door on the rest. I also saw what they were eating. It was not real meat but slops. And for some of these people it can take more than two weeks before they are examined. And for that period of time they are not even allowed to go outside. They live and sleep in what they have on! It's possible to find better clothes in the garbage. But that's not the end of it. They are made to sleep with the lights on. It is such humiliation of these young people, which takes place on the instruction of official organizations. I want to say, isn't it time that the rights of such organizations were limited when they concern the honour and dignity of a human being?

L. Yigora, doctor, Balakova, Saratavsky region.

THERE have been calls for the citizens of the northern regions to support a motion for a nuclear-free and ecologically clean north. I want to tell you, thirty years ago in 1959–60 I worked on vessels of the northern fleet. I participated in some of the voyages. At Zhlanye Cape some shells and bombs were dumped in 512 metres of water together with German-made poisonous gas shells. Even when the bombs were unloaded by the crew, sometimes they were leaking poison and five men were taken to hospital with serious side-effects. As a result, for the unloading procedure we were all equipped with masks.

I want to particularly stress that thirty years ago these bombs were leaking poisonous substances through the threaded plugs. You can imagine what has been happening for the last three decades when, in seawater, these plugs will further corrode.

G. Veshnikov, White Sea.

POISON, would you like to try it? Come to Ufar and try our water. Yesterday they tried to console us. The content of phenol in our water supply system is only between twenty and thirty times higher than the permissible limit. How long have we, our children and grandchildren been drinking it? It was only four days ago that an increased amount of chlorine was added to the phenol and by the smell and taste of the poisonous gas we understood that the water was undrinkable. The citizens rushed to buy juices, lemonade and other drinks.

Half of the citizens – over 500,000 people – were searching for pure water. Soon tanks with water appeared in the streets, thanks to the efforts of the city authorities, but the queues amounted to hundreds of people. The elements are not to blame. All this happened through the irresponsibility of people and those who are responsible for this escaped punishment.

There is one more thing that is worrying. Some laymen on TV are trying to convince us that there is nothing serious, just a stream of phenol that got into the water supply system – 'boil the water and you'll keep healthy and fit.'

How long will it last? It looks like someone invisible is consistently trying to infuriate the people. The numerous decrees, appeals and even laws don't interfere with his criminal activities.

T. Ivanovsky, Ufar.

AFTER the war I remained in the armed forces and then I retired as a captain. I was decorated with three orders and fourteen medals. Then one day I had to appeal to the military committee for help. I asked them to send me to a military hospital for medical treatment. But they refused on the grounds that I was not a major or a lieutenant-colonel. That's why I have a question. Did captains and lieutenants not fight as well as majors at the front? Or could it be that the shells and bullets which wounded us were different than for other ranks?

V. Prooedsa, Kutaisi.

Question and Answer

HOW many candidates and doctors of science are there in the country? Is the number of research institutions and their staff kept within some limits?

A. Selivanov, Kharkov.

According to the USSR State Committee for Statistics there were 5,111 scientific institutions in the country by the end of 1988, staffed by 1,342,000 personnel.

All in all there are 493,000 certified candidates of sciences and 49,700 doctors of science in the USSR.

The largest proportion of certified scientists work in the Russian Federation – 33,400 doctors and 315,600 candidates of science. In the Ukraine there are respectively 6,800 and 73,700; in Uzbekistan 1,400 and 16,700; Byelorussia 1,200 and 14,600; Georgia 1,500 and 11,800 and in Kazakhstan 1,000 and 14,800 – *AIF*.

WHENEVER I go into a chemist's I am invariably met with the retort 'sorry, no cotton wool'. [*Soviet women do not have access to sanitary towels or tampons and are dependent on cotton wool for makeshift towels.*] Why is this the case when we are one of the world's biggest cotton producers?

I. Yelinetskaya, Volgagrad.

L. Relin, vice-chairman of the main department for the cotton industry, replies:

We're not only one of the biggest producers of cotton in the world, but the largest producers of cotton wool. In the past ten years our output has increased from 35.7 thousand tons in 1980 to 49.3 in 1989. There is, however, a shortage of cotton wool in chemists. The main reason is the unpractical use of cotton wool. To contain the wastage we need to pre-pack it. But because we lack the right equipment only 26.7 per cent is pre-packed. If we could start to produce tampons for women we could make a saving of 30,000 tons.

Nowhere in the world is cotton wool used in the quantities that we use here. Because it is so cheap (it is State subsidized) much is used for non-medical purposes, e.g. hairdressers, optical industries, sealing windows, etc.

The problem of cotton wool shortages is due to the scarcity of equipment which we do not manufacture. In December, Gosplan allocated R192 million to the modernization of existing factories in this industry, as well as for the construction of four new factories.

CAN you give us some recent information on suicide rates in the Soviet Union? Is suicide on the increase?

G. Asmolov, Komi, ASSR.

Information provided by USSR State Statistics Committee and O. Sestrensky:

In 1988 there were 77,000 deaths caused by suicide and murder, which represent 27 per cent of the total number of deaths by misfortune, poisoning and injury. According to the information we have so far, there were 87,000 suicides and murders in 1989, which represent 30 per cent of the overall total.

Following a noticeable drop in the numbers of suicides and murders in 1985 and 1986, the figures for the next two years remained fairly stable. The latest figures show an increase in 1989:

	Thousands		Per 100,000 population	
Year	Murders	Suicides	Murders	Suicides
1984	24	81	9	30
1985	21	68	8	25
1986	16	53	6	19
1987	17	54	6	19
1988	21	56	7	19
1989*	27	60	10	21

* Provisional figures.

The suicide rate in Great Britain is 9 per 100,000 of population. In the US it is 12, in West Germany 21 and in France 22.

In 1988, 2.8 times more men were murdered in the USSR than women, 3.3 times more men ended their own lives, and in the 25 to 39 age group, this figure rose to 4 and 6 times respectively.

Ninety per cent of murders of males and 80 per cent of male suicides occur during their younger, working years, whereas with women over half of the suicides (54 per cent) and about one third of murders (31 per cent) occur later in life.

In the republics the suicide rate ranges from 2 to 8 per 100,000 of population in the Caucasian and Central Asian republics (with the exception of Kirgizia), up to 23 to 26 per 100,000 in the Russian Federation and the Baltic republics. The Russian Federation has the highest rate. Moldavia and Kazakhstan have 10–7 per 100,000, and Tajikistan and the Caucasian republics have less with 2–3 per 100,000.

There is a direct link between the high suicide rate and alcohol abuse. At the present time there are 4.6 million registered alcoholics undergoing treatment, which is three times as many as there were in 1970. Every year 0.4–0.5 million people register as alcoholics in the Soviet Union.

| | Murders | | Suicides | |
	Men	Women	Men	Women
Total deaths	11.3	4.1	30.8	9.3
Under age 20	2.1	1.1	4.1	1.5
20–24	14.7	3.2	22.5	5.6
25–29	20.1	4.7	34.4	5.6
30–39	21.2	6.1	43.8	7.2
40–49	16.9	6.5	54.8	11.5
50–59	12.4	5.1	54.9	14.8
60–69	9.2	4.6	48.2	17.6
70 and older	10.9	6.1	75.5	27.7

IN January 1989 under a new decree, five State-owned dachas (country houses) outside Moscow were handed over to children's sanatoria. Can you tell us more about this?

G. Polynev, Zagorsk.

D. Gurov answers:

Yes, you are right; on 29 January 1989 the KGB 9th Division handed over five State-owned dachas to the USSR Ministry of Health. The houses are several kilometres outside Moscow on the Altufevsk highway and stand in 200 hectares (494 acres) of land, a lovely green belt, only marginally spoiled by the construction of the Northern Electric Power Station nearby. The houses have had famous occupants like Voroshilov, Kirilenko, Eduard Sheverdnadze, Boris Yeltsin, Zaikov, Mrs Biryukova and others.

Now the new owners have taken over. Voroshilov and Sheverdnadze's State dachas are being used by children suffering from diabetes. They have sixty hectares (282 acres) of land attached to them. One of the wings that used to house guards and service personnel is now being renovated and turned into a clinic.

Under the Ministry of Health decree dated 22.02.90, the State dacha which until recently was used by the Moscow party's First Secretary, Mr Zaikov, was transferred into the hands of the Institute for Children's Oncology. The Institute's director, Professor Durnov, said, 'I am constantly being asked whether the children we have here aren't being singled out for special treatment. It costs us R25 a day to treat a child here, but I don't think we should be measuring everything in financial terms. Dostoyevsky wrote that "none of the riches of the world are worth the tears of one child." We are expecting our first intake of children early in the summer.'

No one has yet decided what Mrs Biryukova's dacha is going to be used for and it is still standing empty.

In Russia they say that it is better to have seen something once with one's eyes rather than have heard about it a hundred times. Marshal Voroshilov's dacha was built specially for him in 1932 and was rebuilt in 1952 after being damaged by fire. It stands on 1,000 square metres of land. The 'first Red officer' used to like jumping his favourite horse in through the window of the room adjacent to his bedroom. More recently this dacha was occupied by A. P. Kirilenko.

The Western-style two-storey country house was made over to the Soviet Foreign Minister in 1981. According to local people, it was mostly his relations who lived there. Their only problem was that they didn't manage to stay there long enough to swim in their private swimming pool. It would appear that even ministers and their families suffer from the vagaries of builders who take too long over jobs.

Not only was this dacha protected from the outside world by the marble lions at its entrance, but by double layers of barbed wire draped over the top of the garden walls, by electronic surveillance equipment and thirty burly young men who were on constant patrol. There was good reason for all this security. The sixty-three hectares (155 acres) of land contained the villa itself, built early this century (with a lift to take you up to the second floor). There was also a two-storey house for the service personnel and guards, a seventeen-by-four-metre swimming pool and greenhouses. Not to mention a pond full of carp of various sorts. The bomb shelter goes down to a depth of twelve metres. And this is not all. A conservative estimate of the value of this dacha would be about R2 million, and together with its land, this would be about R4.5 million. The estate's chandeliers alone are worth several thousand roubles.

We are still not sure what is to happen to many of these dachas. On the assumption that the regulation square footage per child (currently at maximum 0.1 hectare [0.25 acre] per child) is being exceeded, the Central Architectural and Planning Directorate is not letting any more go at present. Which means that there are dachas standing empty with various organizations arguing over them, while locals carry off bits of their garden fences to mend their own, leaving yawning gaps as long as ten to fifteen metres in places. The swimming pool's pump has already mysteriously disappeared, as have several nice rugs from the main house. Is this how we 'do our best for our children'?

THE table below was made up using information provided by the USSR State Committee for the Natural Environment and the US Trade Department's Economic Analysis Bureau.

Expenditure on Environmental Protection in USSR and USA in 1987 (billions dollars).

	Total	Air	Water	Solid Waste
USSR	16.28	2.08	10.3	—
USA	81.06	31.8	32.5	16.7

In absolute terms we spend at least five times less than the Americans on ecological measures (using the official Soviet rouble-dollar exchange rate for our calculations). If we take into account the actual purchasing power of these two currencies, then this difference becomes even greater. Yet we are physically a larger country than the USA and have a larger population, so that logically we should be spending more on ecological measures than they are. We spend 1.6 per cent of GNP on environmental protection; in the States this figure is 2.2 per cent.

The actual structure of expenditure is also different. Both countries spend most on current and major projects to clean up water (we spend over half of all environmental budgets on this, the USA spends 40.1 per cent). But the most dynamic item in the American environmental budget is the money spent on destroying and rendering harmless solid waste products, which have been mounting up alarmingly fast in recent years. The Soviet Union doesn't spend anything on this at all. And this despite the fact that solid waste products are the largest potential source of environmental pollution. Add to this the fact that the Americans spend an annual $2.3–$2.6 billion on environmental research and development, and that we have no idea how much the Soviet Union spends in this area.

The main brunt of environmental protection expenditure in the Soviet Union is borne by our long-suffering State budget. The main source of environmental pollution is State-owned enterprises. Only about 2 per cent of all investment in Soviet industry goes on environmental protection measures, while this figure is 4 to 5 per cent in the USA, and even higher in Japan. Overall the private sector in the US pays for exactly half of all anti-pollution measures. In West Germany this is 37 per cent and in the United Kingdom 25 per cent.

One of the results of growing expenditure on environmental protection in the West has been the appearance of a large market for ecotechnology and the appearance of a whole multi-million-dollar industry producing anti-pollution equipment. The environmental clean-up campaign has led to an economic growth area. There are no ecotechnology markets or industries so far in the Soviet Union.

The Soviet Union has set aside R3.3 billion for ecological programmes in 1990. But this is not all. In the interests of ecology and protecting the environment, a whole range of industries will have to be cut back and we will have to stop producing and using certain types of product. This can frequently lead to a clash between traditional material demands and ecological requirements.

The West has a certain amount of experience in predicting situations of this kind, although even here it is by no means always easy to choose between the needs of the environment and the demands of the public. The first thing they do is to make the widest use of available ecological expertise when planning any economic project. In addition, almost any group of people has the right to challenge any project in court.

However, the only way to really make a major change in the way we link ecological and economic requirements is to start thinking countrywide about a fundamentally new model of how we use natural resources and the environment. This model should be based on making sure that production units are sensibly located, that we rationalize our use of natural resources and at the same time install and use ecologically clean technologies.

B. Maklyarsky, candidate of economic sciences.

THERE are cases of leprosy in the USSR. How many are there altogether? And do we have hospitals for them?

G. D. Busygin, Krasnodar.

A. Binev answers:

There is leprosy in the USSR but it is decreasing. In the last ten years annually only twelve to fifteen new cases were registered. Taking into account the reduction, it is believed that by the year 2000 the number of patients will be 2,250 with an average age of more than forty. In the initial stages of this illness it's possible to cure it but when the illness develops it's necessary to treat people till the end of their lives. Those cured remain under medical control. At present out of 4,000 affected people more than 3,000 have completed a successful course of treatment. There are around 1,000 people in hospital. The highest number of cases occurred in Karakalpatska autonomous republic, Zhyl-Arginski region, Kazalskia republic and also along the Volga, Don, Amurdaria and Sirdaria rivers. Seventy per cent of those in hospital are disabled which is why, apart from the medical treatment, they receive social care, pensions and material support. There are sixteen anti-leprosy establishments in the USSR but none of them has hospitals attached. The biggest of these are in Astrakhan – Astrakhanski Scientific Research Institute on Leprosy Studies – Tserski, Abinsky and Khazakski. In each of them there are from 80–150 beds. There are fifteen million leprosy patients in the world, mainly in India and the countries of Southeast Asia and Africa.

HOW many Aids patients are there in the Soviet Union and what measures are being taken to combat this ominous disease?

T. Sarzhin, Chelyabinsk.

A. Konrusev, Chief State Sanitary Inspector and Deputy Health Minister, answers:

To date eleven Aids cases have been identified, including four children (two of whom died). The Human Immunodeficiency Virus (HIV) has been found in 289 Soviet citizens, including 115 children and 393 foreigners, who have been deported from the USSR. The geographic range of

113

HIV infection has likewise broadened. Carriers have now been registered in eight Union republics. In the world as a whole there are 157,191 recorded cases of Aids in 149 countries.

In order to maintain a check on Aids, a nationwide screening campaign is under way in the country to find those who are infected with HIV. More than thirty-two million have been examined in the USSR. To prevent the virus spreading via donor blood, more than twenty million donors were examined. Eight people were found to be infected with HIV.

A total of eighty million non-convertible and three million convertible roubles have been allocated for Aids research in 1989. A drug currently used to treat Aids cases is azidotimidin which improves the general condition but, unfortunately, does not cure the disease fully.

HOW is currency spent in the health services?
A. Moptorin, Orenburg region.

V. Gromyko, Soviet Deputy Health Minister replies:

Currency for the purchase of medical equipment and instruments is allocated by the USSR Council of Ministers. Over recent years the sum has remained practically unchanged. In 1988 it amounted to some 38.4 million convertible roubles. It is the Health Ministry Collegium that distributes this sum between the various health services.

A total of 14,373,000 convertible roubles was spent on equipment for diagnostic centres and R551,200 was earmarked for the USSR Research Institute of Medical Equipment to carry out tests. 1,135,000,000 convertible roubles worth of medicines was purchased abroad in 1988.

REPORTEDLY infant mortality has grown in the USSR. Could you give us the statistics?
S. Abdurakhmanova, Chirchik, Uzbekistan.

According to the Soviet Health Ministry 142,200 or twenty-five per 1,000 new-born children died in the Soviet Union in 1987.

The highest infant mortality was in Turkmenia, Tajikistan

and Uzbekistan – fifty-six, forty-nine and forty-six per 1,000 respectively. The lowest death rate was in Latvia and Lithuania.

Among the main causes of infant mortality were respiratory diseases: seventy-nine per 10,000 new-born children (240–264 per 10,000 in Central Asia and Azerbaijan), and infectious diseases: forty-four per 10,000 on average (180 per 10,000 in Central Asia and seven to nine in the Baltics).

As many as 188,000, or 4 per cent, of all pregnant women gave birth to premature babies. The death rate among premature babies is twelve times higher than average.

The number of women who smoke (up to thirty years old) has almost reached 40 per cent and as many as 30 per cent of women who drink give birth to premature babies.

I have heard that the Soviet Union is near the top of the world list as regards the number of abortions. Is anything being done to improve this obviously abnormal situation?

I. Gorobovsky, Kishinev.

Until recently abortions were practically the only means of avoiding an unwanted pregnancy. The following data from the USSR Ministry of Health provide enough evidence of this: in 1986 for each 100 births there were 120 abortions; in 1987, 115. There are still backstreet abortions: in 1987 they constituted 12.1 per cent of the total number of abortions carried out in the country. In Moscow every other woman terminates all subsequent pregnancies after the birth of her first child; every fourth terminates her first pregnancy.

Why is there such a high number of abortions? We asked the head of the USSR Ministry of Health's Department of Therapeutic and Prophylactic Medical Aid for the Mother and Child, V. Alekseev, to answer this question and to comment upon the figures quoted above:

Firstly, the situation is caused by insufficient public information and by the often unfounded fear of the effects brought about by the use of contraception. It has to be said that the work of the information and advisory service on birth control has been far from satisfactory. We are perfectly able to provide an efficient and competent family planning service. For over ten years now we have been promoting the use of the intra-uterine contraceptive device which is 97–99 per cent effective and complications following insertion are extremely rare. Unfortunately our industry does not produce sufficient supplies of IUDs.

Recently we have started buying hormonal contraceptives from other Comecon countries. According to the USSR Ministry of Health there is no need to worry. The requirements of medical institutions for hormonal contraceptives are being met in full. Women who wish to use them can do so providing there are no contra-indications. They only have to see their doctor who will write a prescription.

This is the theory . . . in practice? The head of District Department No. 9 of the Moscow Women's Clinic, gynaecologist Y. Dadalova, explains:

Women very rarely seek consultancy in these matters. When a doctor recommends a hormonal contraceptive the first reaction is always the same. 'But these are bad for you and I will put on a lot of weight.' It is true that in the past we did not have reliable contraceptives but now we do women still refuse to use them. To a certain extent the fault lies with the doctors. There are family planning clinics where the doctors do not even know the names of available contraceptives.

(Like everything else, condoms are in desperately short supply. And the home-produced ones are widely distrusted. 'Perfect,' a young Muscovite told me, 'when you use three at once.' The prostitutes who ply the hard-currency bars of the large hotels insist on Western ones – I'm told – Ed.)

116

CHAPTER FOUR

ECONOMY AND AGRICULTURE

The average Soviet wage is around R240 a month. In Brezhnev's 'period of stagnation' when there were plenty of goods in the shops, the average Soviet citizen had a high disposable income. The move to the market economy – and gross shortages and spiralling prices – means this is becoming less true today. The subsistence minimum per person in the late 1980s has been calculated at R85 and it is estimated that at least one-fifth (more than seventy million) of the Soviet people live below the poverty line. About half of these are in large families, chiefly in Central Asia, Kazakhstan and Azerbaijan: young families account for around one-third and pensioners the rest.

The Soviet economy grew massively in the fifties, sixties and seventies but fell back sharply in the eighties in spite of continuously high rates of investment. A reason for this – as Gorbachev has expounded on – is abysmally inefficient production and management in both industry and agriculture (where over a quarter of the annual harvest moulders). But the defence race has virtually bankrupted the country as well as inhibited the development of the industrial economy. Until last year 75 per cent of all budget allocations on research and development went on military-related research programmes. The budget deficit is estimated at 11–14 per cent, compared with the supposedly drastic budget deficit of the USA which is about 3 per cent.

The USSR has traditionally been a major provider of aid to the

*developing world, although this is now being cut back: in the early
eighties Soviet aid was 1.3 per cent of GNP, more than five times
that of the US and in 1986 this figure was 1.7 per cent.*

*In 1985 the value of an average family's personal property was
R7,300: 11.6 per cent of this was for motor vehicles, 31 per cent
clothes and footwear, and household articles 28.2 per cent. By
comparison, in 1984 in the USA the value of the average family's
personal property was $32,700, about R200,000.*

I want to give President Gorbachev a piece of advice. Please
invite Margaret Thatcher to be appointed chairman of the
Council of Ministers of the USSR. Do I need to explain? I
don't think it's necessary! However, I'd like to add a few
words. Our premier Nikolai Ivanovich Ryzhkov might be a
good man but in this most complicated period of our history
he doesn't seem to be a person who can foresee the rapidly
developing events in this country and cope with the problems
arising. In this respect the Iron Lady, who has been determining the policy and the economic life of Great Britain for over
ten years, doesn't need any recommendation.

But would Margaret Thatcher agree? I'd like to believe she
would. People of such fate and character, of such great
efficiency in their sphere of activities, always strive for the
solution of the most difficult problems so one can hope that
Margaret Thatcher might accept this proposal. She might
consider it to be interesting.

E. Trespisnikov.

*(Like most things in the Soviet Union, gems and jewellery are
sold by the State, through State shops, to the people. Rather
than trust the 'wooden rouble' many put their savings into
jewellery. But precious metals are also a major investment of 'the
mafia', the criminals and speculators who have proliferated in the
black economy – Ed.)*

ON 9 January 1990 our government increased the price of
gold, silver and precious stones by 50 per cent. Detailed
reasons were not given but they are required. Think about it.

No one knows how many items of gold and other valuable metals are held by Soviet citizens. But through this price increase something like R2.5 billion was to be raised to put towards pensions. But, has nobody taken into account that the value of precious items in the hands of individuals has now increased by half. With all of this we increased by 50 per cent the wealth of our underground and half-legal millionaires.

Since the sixties, gold and similar items have gone up by more than fifteen times. So someone then who had R1,000 worth of jewellery now has R15,000 worth. Can we justify dividing our people into rich and poor for the sake of R2.5 billion for our respected pensioners? If we had increased prices on black and red caviare and other luxury goods which the people almost never see – and many people don't even know the names of – this would not have resulted in the further enrichment of our rich.

P. Mikhailovsky, Novosibirsk.

LET this letter be the expression of my most grateful thanks to the Council of Ministers, and particularly to Comrade Ryzhkov, for raising the price of gold by 50 per cent. This move has immediately made us, businessmen of shady dealings (as we are usually called), one and a half times richer. I already suspected that some of our people were in government. Now I know it. In raising the price of gold, the Council of Ministers must have known that the destitute will remain destitute. On the other hand we, the wealthy ones, will no longer possess a few paltry gold items; instead we shall be able to assess our wealth in kilograms of gold. Also, we don't need to queue in jewellers' shops to buy golden trinkets. Our gold comes to us by different routes. How? No need to go into details. Many thanks to the government for the new tax law. It will help us to get rid of the competition, all those co-operative businessmen and other agents. Thank you, thank you! This government will look after me. Clearly our interests coincide.

I have written this letter to show that our faithful trust in the 'Good Soviet Tsar' was not without grounds. And not without reason do the Soviet people exchange one regional party secretary for another, instead of sending them all packing. Our only concern now is for our successors, who will continue our cause. For money, you can buy everything in our country – from a plot at a cemetery to exemption from a prison sentence. Not to mention jobs and positions.

P. Koreiko, undercover millionaire.

I read a letter published in *Argumenty i Fakty* in which a Moscow teacher asked 'how much concrete has been wasted upon those reinforced-concrete nightmare houses during the past thirty years . . . ?' I have the answer to this question: it involves a number of negative phenomena which took place during the years of stagnation. One of them concerns turning out shoddy and worthless goods. It is enough to say that the amount of metal in reinforced concrete used nowadays for the construction of prefabricated building elements would in itself suffice to build all-metal houses, without any concrete . . . Thus, overall losses of metal used in mass production of reinforced concrete for prefabricated buildings amount to over fifty million tons. Fifty million cars could be made out of this amount of steel; cars which would bring a profit of R500 billion – like they do in all developed countries. However, the opportunity to considerably augment the national revenue was missed. It was buried, with the metal, in concrete. So were other materials: cement, road-metal, sand and fuel.

Indeed, for many years the labour of five million people was wasted, too. In fact, even according to very low estimates, thirty years of the 'reinforced-concrete policy' in capital construction has cost the country no less than R700 billion. The same amount as the 1941–45 war!

In England, the total proportion of non-traditional construction work is 6 per cent. There, reinforced-concrete buildings built from prefabricated elements were ultimately rejected both by the government and the public, and the construction companies involved went bankrupt.

Prefabricated reinforced-concrete constructions have not been welcomed with open arms in the USA either. There are two construction companies in the state of Florida which still turn out reinforced-concrete houses made from prefabricated elements. However, they are no longer used in industrial construction. Our building workers, who still carry out their worthless task, are being legally paid for their work. Their pay comes from the Wages Fund (approximately R100 billion) as well as from public consumption funds (approximately R30 billion).

V. Orlyansky, research worker.

OUR mass media applauded the decision by the Federal German Republic to give us DM220 million to purchase meat and other products. Yes, it seems wonderful. The big power, with a population of almost 300 million, with vast lands, with enormous resources of raw materials, takes this charity. It has been common from ancient times for one leader to give gifts to another. It used to be horses and now it's currency to purchase meat. But why? Isn't this just payment for our agreement to German reunification?

So, I compared this with another piece of information which I got from a recent issue of *Communist* magazine. Among all the enterprises controlled by the Ministry of Chemical and Petroleum Industry and the State gas corporation, there is foreign-made equipment, not yet installed, which cost R1.2 billion. And now these organizations are holding talks about establishing nine big joint ventures with foreign companies. The planned expenditure is $17 billion. More than that, the Vnesheconombank [*State economic bank*] says that it these fail then our country will carry the entire burden. There are many other examples like this. Not only do the people have to pay financially, but by our national and State dignity. Shame on us. It's intensely bitter to realize that we are squandering the enormous resources and richness of our country – and we are happy when we get such gifts.

D. Madeuz, dean of philisophy, Minsk State Teachers Institute of Foreign Languages.

(*In many areas, particularly rural ones, attempts have been made to recycle materials and some have become commodities in themselves, with some unfortunate side-effects – Ed.*)

TO buy a television set we, a newly married couple, had to pay with thirty kilos of non-ferrous metal. We saw a large vessel in the shop which weighed nine kilos. We bought three of them; we crushed them and added a few pans which we also crushed.

To buy shoes, or anything else for that matter, you have to give metals, rags, paper, wool or pork. It is the only way. So, somewhere there is a plant manufacturing useful vessels and the people are crushing them. Another instance is the shop here which sells mattresses and they are bought and destroyed for rags. Similarly, whether or not you are a good or bad writer, under such conditions your books are snapped up as soon as they are published – for waste paper.

And what about pork? Recently our village received a lot of shoes and for three kilos of pork you could buy a pair. Everyone rushed to the store and bought pork – me too. Then I had to take the pork to the so-called procurement office (to get a voucher for the shoes). From here my pork was taken back to the store. Then the next buyer purchases the same piece of pork and takes it to the procurement office . . . and then the next buyer . . . !

Perhaps this is all very profitable for the State. I buy a pair of shoes and at the same time two or three mattresses – it doesn't matter to the State that I destroyed them because, nevertheless, I paid for them. But should it be done this way? It would interest me to know if this happens throughout our country . . . and who was the intelligent person who invented this system?

                    T. Maslavoyava, villager, Vidipsk region, Byelorussia.

(Income Tax in the Soviet Union is only paid on salaries exceeding the average [about R240 a month], but the tax, 13 per cent, is then levied on the whole amount. As are other 'taxes' – Ed.)

I am a candidate of sciences and a chief technologist. My monthly salary is R415. From this sum I pay 13 per cent – R53.95 – as tax and 1 per cent as trade union dues, R4.15. That's why I actually receive R356.9. The Communist party dues are taken at 3 per cent, R12.45, from the total sum and not after other deductions. On the basis of this CPSU members are paying dues on taxes and also on trade union fees. On wages and salaries which are not as big as mine it might not be so noticeable. Isn't it high time we changed the CPSU rules?

A. Kirimov, Ali Baramli, Azerbaijan.

WE live in Timertao, a satellite town of Karagandar, where there is a rather well-known Karagandar sweet factory working to full capacity. But we aren't surprised nowadays that there are no sweets from this factory in our shops. However, how can it possibly be that there are sweets from the Almatar factory [*the other side of the country*]? The same thing with detergents. Nearby us is the Shartinsky plant but we get detergents from the Baltic republics with our coupons. Can you find even any sense in this in the new self-accounting system that is being introduced everywhere?

I wonder how much money was spent on the transportation to and fro of detergents and sweets and all the rest? And how much all of this adds up to across the whole of the country?

Y. Ilina, Khazakska.

IN all the imperialist countries the banks are paying to their account holders 'real interest'. These rates are set to attract accounts and they cover the inflation factor. This is beneficial to the banks, which can use the money deposited profitably, and also to the people who put the money in the bank who are sure that their savings will not only not be devalued by inflation but can actually increase due to the interest they receive. In our country all the banks give only 2 per cent interest annually. If it is short-term investment then 3 per cent. With the level of inflation at 9–10 per cent it means that only our dear State is using the savings of the population profitably.

It's even investing in galloping inflation and the erosion of all these savings. Taking into account that most of the savings are rather small sums of money, saved over many years from small wages and salaries for a 'rainy day', then it becomes clear that it is an intentional robbing of the people by the State through this inflation. As the savings of the people are melting, the time will come when there is nothing left.

N. Vasilkov, pensioner, Moscow.

THE conversion of defence industry factories to the manufacture of consumer goods led recently to more than forty of those firms approaching our Krasnodar Design Bureau and Technological Institute to ask us to work out designs and documentation on products they were manufacturing: sideshow and funfair rides. It's good because in this country there is a chronic shortage of such attractions and the production at the present level is not even enough for the replacement of those which are out of order. The people who maintain these sideshows say they are a lucrative meal ticket because in a year they can earn more repairing them than they actually cost.

However, despite these rather powerful enterprises moving into this area the situation is not going to change a lot in the near future because of the taxation position. Although there is no tax on the actual production itself, the design services and scientific assistance are heavily taxed. And that's why it was not possible for our institute to take orders from the companies. So while companies are being pushed and encouraged into different areas on the one hand, on the other hand there are heavy State disincentives. Where is the sense?

J. G., scientist.

I read a statement from Academician Ginsburg that there are one million State cars for personal use in our country. Their maintenance costs from R8–10 billion annually. Isn't it true that each personal car is maintained by two or three people? Driver – even two drivers – mechanical workers, fitters and others in the garage, and so on. If each of those had actually worked producing something they could have created the materials they are using (goods and services).

Taking into account the total gross national product and the number of working people in our country, on average each person generates about R1,000 a month, approximately

R10,000 a year. Multiply this by the estimated two million people involved in keeping these State cars functioning and we would get R20 billion annually. That's the lowest estimate. And what kind of income would be generated to the State if all those garages and workshops were rented out or changed over to production?

The argument that labour productivity is increased from the people who have such cars is doubtful. It's clear that a certain number of cars should be left at the ministries and other organizations but let us say 100–200,000, not more. Even in this case it would be possible, at the lowest estimate, to save R24–27 billion a year. And if we take the one-time profits of the sale of such cars at auction then this total sum would be much higher.

Professor A. Garilek, Moscow.

(*The shortage of cars in the USSR and the demand for them is legendary. The logic and the mathematical formulae in the following letter may not make a lot of sense in the West, predicated on the assumption that every worker, every year wants to buy a new car! Consider, however, that a second-hand car in the USSR can often cost more than a new one. Why? The new one has a State-controlled price [an average Lada would cost R10,000, although it's true that the State has now started to auction its new cars], the old one doesn't and its price floats on the market – Ed.*)

IT'S well known that it's not possible to freely buy a car in our country. First of all they are distributed among different ministries and organizations and then among different plants and factories. However, even with this situation we should have the principle of social justice. If the number of working people in the USSR (approximately 140 million) is divided by the number of new cars a year (approximately 800,000) then the result is the number of people standing in a queue to buy one car. The queue is 175 people.

We have a letter from the Ministry of Electrical and Technical Instruments where it is said that their ministry receives one car per 850 employees. That means five times less than average. Perhaps this ministry doesn't work well and is punished in this way. However, in our talks with the chief of one of the departments of the Ministry of Trade of the USSR, A. Spesitsov, the following average figure was given for all branches: 1.19 cars per 1,000 employees. Or 840 people to one car. It means also that it's five times lower than the average.

It is known in Moscow that 30,000 cars are sold annually. Let us assume that five million people are working in Moscow. It means one car is sold per 167 people. So that we make things balance it means that some enterprises receive twenty times more cars than others! And what are they? Why do they have such privileges? Who decides how many should be given and to whom? The Council of Ministers, the Ministry of Trade of the USSR? This is unknown and it is kept as a great secret.

B. Rodin, deputy director; A. Tikhanov, chairman of the trade unions; B. Sakhalov, chairman of the staff, Scientific Research Institute, Moscow.

(*The State has traditionally divided workers into two categories, A and B. A workers, given priority and resources, were involved in the creation of the 'means of production', B workers in producing-consumer goods – Ed.*)

WE recall very clearly the failure of reform in 1965 with great sadness. How did it happen? I'll tell you how it happened in our design institute. Our director was called to the district party committee and told to begin the work in a new way. How much will you earn? It depends on you. We will give you a bonus on your wages and salaries and let you work as you want. For example, the salary of an engineer was R100–120. They could earn up to R150 but to earn more was impossible. Over that the bonus rate was reduced. Now we were promised that these wouldn't be reduced if we worked harder.

What happened you can't imagine. Even the worst engineer started to do four and even five times normal work and received R500, even R600 a month. And the reform continued for a whole two months! And then suddenly, and unexpectedly, everything stopped. The director was called back to the district party committee and was asked, 'What is happening at your institute? Everything has become crazy.

126

We don't have enough money to pay for this. No one should do more than 150 per cent of the norm, otherwise there is no money for pay.' And from that time on we started to quietly work 150 per cent of the norm, not more.

So why are we talking about all this restructuring now? There is no money in the bank to carry out these reforms. Is that clear? Why there is no money is another question. Let us think about it. Perhaps it is necessary to change the ratio between groups A and B of workers in order to store up consumer goods. But one thing is certain, in 1965 it wasn't the lack of democracy but a lack of money. Again it's exactly the same. There are no goods to buy with the money we already have.

And foreigners tell us 'your people in the villages, on the land could earn R50,000 a year.' But even if it became so, what would they do with all that money when there is nothing to buy? It's all the same to us. No one will consider this until people stop working again, because there are no incentives for them to work.

V. Suslov, Chelyabinsk

BEFORE retiring on a pension all of my wages would go to the bank for a rainy day – no matter how difficult it was for me and my family. Now the 1960 value of the rouble is worth only forty kopecks. The State has also told us that the savings bank is the best place to keep money – but how is it going to compensate me for my losses?

B. Kharitonov, war and labour veteran, Moscow.

THE city of Dunaevtsy is situated on the Khmelnitsky-Kamenets-Podolsky highway. Alongside a well-developed network of roads there are two railway stations eighteen kilometres from the city: Dunaevtsy, in the direction of Khmelnitsky, and Balin, in the direction of Kamenets-Podolsky. In other words, the region's transport system allows free travel of goods and cargoes. Yet all shops in the city belong to co-ops (not State ones).

Presumably co-ops buy meat, milk, vegetables and fruits from the locals, something that may explain the higher prices. But what about biscuits, pasta, other foodstuffs, consumer goods and durables produced by State-run enterprises? Why should I pay R7.09 for an electric hotplate instead of R7 as in the rest of the country? Or R101.20 for a pair of Rifle jeans instead of R100? Do co-ops also buy Rifle jeans from local residents?

The authorities say that the extra charge stems from transport problems. This is ridiculous: Kamenets-Podolsky is a long way from Dunaevtsy but prices there are the same as elsewhere. Therefore, earning R250 a month, people in Dunaevtsy and in Kamenets-Podolsky have different standards of living.

I'm not much of an economist but, obviously, transportation costs are pretty much the same in Dunaevtsy as in Khmelnitsky or Kamenets-Podolsky. If so, why should we pay extra?

A. Filippov, Dunaevtsy, Khmelnitskiy region.

At the Danyets metallurgy plant the first continuous casting mill in the world was commissioned thirty years ago, which saves approximately 15–20 per cent of steel. Foreign delegations came to us and the Soviet State sold licences on this unit to them. And for the past thirty years Japanese and German people have used continuous casting for their steel and they cast almost all of it this way.

Only 20 per cent of our steel is cast this way. Why is this? We invented this technology, we developed it, we designed it and we have given it all away and ended up behind the rest of the world.

What does this mean for the whole USSR? One hundred and sixty million tons of steel is cast in our country and if we had the continuous casting then 120–130 million tons would be enough because, anyway, the rest goes to waste. Apart from this it would not be necessary to cast sixteen million tons of iron, and to get ten million tons of coke from twenty million tons of coal, sixty million tons of ore. How many raw materials have we lost over the last thirty years? The ecological conditions have been made worse due to the mode of steel casting we're using now.

Y. Kulikov, chairman of the Dnepropetrovsk regional committee of the veterans of war and labour.

HOW much did one metre of the Iron Curtain cost to build?

P. P., Moscow.

IT is a pity that we're selling our raw materials mainly abroad – oil, petroleum, gas, ore, coal and so on – as if our country was a developing one. It would not have been so regrettable if we had been selling surpluses. Our newspapers are telling us that we have shortages of petroleum in industry and agriculture and they also tell of our losses on this. Many experience the shortage of gas. For instance here in our region of Baku-Achmidlie people do not have hot water because of this and in villages and settlements – especially in the mountains – the population is using wood to heat the stoves. If our country cannot provide its own population with oil, petroleum and gas why should we export all this for kopecks?

If there is sense in all this then let those responsible explain it to the people.

G. Khelev, Baku.

I suggest an issue of 'new' money alongside that currently in use at the ratio of 1:1. Not additionally, but as part of the quantity now in circulation, i.e. through emission or renewal of banknotes. The 'new' money would be backed by sought-after goods which should be sold in all stores – but for 'new' money only. This would remove the need for rationing, making it harder for forgers and black-market dealers. Within a few years this money would force the 1961 banknotes out of circulation, setting the scene for a monetary reform that would not impinge on the interest of working people.

M. Gorban, Kiev.

HOW can we speak of the lack of grain if we waste twenty-nine million tons every year? Why did we buy alcoholic and other drinks worth R248 m. in 1987 and R224 m. in 1988 abroad while cutting down our own vineyards? For whom have we imported fifty-five billion cigarettes?

I. Suchkov, Vologda.

I remember 1952–56 when we were forced to take out government bonds. My husband got R600 a month in old currency and I got R500. Besides ourselves we had two children and two old people to support. To make both ends meet I decided to refuse to subscribe to the bond and for this I was not allowed to continue working. It was only when I paid my salary for the loan that I was allowed to return to work.

My husband and I have been working for forty-nine years and our pensions are scanty. We want to get our money back but the government doesn't seem to be in a hurry. They are waiting for us to die. As for our grandchildren they will say 'it's none of your business . . . what have you got to do with it?' The Ministry of Finance says there is no money but we believe it's necessary to find the money otherwise all this talk about social justice is nothing but empty words. Something can be done. To begin with, in return for the bonds they could give us savings bank books so that those who possess them could withdraw, say, fifteen or twenty roubles a year. It's no secret that most of the bonds have already been lost, so the government will know how many bonds the population has in its possession. Probably the government can afford to pay their debt after all.

Sinyakova, Chelyabinsk.

I have had direct experience of the USSR Ministry of Finance's regulations relating to holders of foreign currency accounts and USSR Vnesheconombank. In my opinion only the narrowest-minded clerk could have dreamed up a set of regulations like this, or somebody who wanted to have some fun at the expense of others. I will use myself as an example. Five of us sold the licence on our invention to the Yugoslavs, for which we were paid R89 each in hard currency. A year later we were given our Vnesheconombank account numbers. Then my money, or should I say, what was left of my money since nobody of course sells a licence abroad for R400, fell into the clutches of the above-mentioned regulations.

Vnesheconombank explained that if I wanted to buy something in a Beriozka shop [*foreign currency only*], I had to get an invoice, take it to Vnesheconombank, waste several hours there on paperwork, go back to the shop and, if the thing I wanted had meanwhile been sold, go all the way back to the bank and undo the process.

In the case of somebody who is not well or who is disabled (like me), then the person who is going to do all this for him or her must 1) have written permission from him or her to act as proxy, 2) written permission to deal with the bank, 3) written permission to receive the money. And if I need to buy something in the foreign currency pharmacy, I have to apply for permission right to the top, to Mr Pavlov the Finance Minister himself.

I would like to ask the Minister when he is going to stop whittling away at our little bits of foreign currency income from selling authors' rights, when he is going to stop making us the butt of his jokes with his regulations, when he is going to at last allow people to receive their own few hard-earned pennies?

S. Vasiliev, disabled war and labour veteran, Moscow.

IT'S no secret nowadays that the main cause of our economic disaster is the separation of the worker from the results of his work. It also concerns the work of inventors. The whole of humanity is indebted to them for technological progress. The shelves of our patent libraries are full of inventions expropriated by the government. Most of those inventions remain on paper and were never used to promote technological progress in our country. Meanwhile our enterprises continue producing outdated goods. It's common knowledge that on the world markets they value high-quality goods and up-to-date technology which guarantees the effectiveness of labour productivity and high quality.

Under the new law on inventions, the draft of which was recently published, the author seemingly becomes the owner of his invention. As is the case in all countries which appreciate that it's not profitable cooking the chicken which lays the golden eggs. Alas this is just an illusion striving to preserve the ruinous monopoly of the State on the intellect – the authors of the draft law evidently remembered that our inventor can't afford to pay the patent dues.

Only one person can give birth to a baby and only one

person can give birth to an idea. An enterprise is unlikely to be a sponsor of its own inventor. There is only one way out of the situation. The inventor will have to put his own orders on other people's banners as before. So again he will remain one in the group of people working under guidance. He will deprive himself of his legitimate right voluntarily.

Vassilev, Kharkov.

THE reports from the international Leipzig trade fair revealed that one of the biggest sites there belongs to the USSR. I have been wondering – what are we showing? Our industries don't fulfil their plans. Otherwise there wouldn't be such a shortage of television sets, refrigerators and washing machines. If we are the largest participant, possessing the largest pavilion, then we should sign big contracts. But no information is given that we have done. It is evident that the exhibition displays things that are not on sale in our country, or they are sold in very small quantities. If so, what's the use of spending money on the construction of pavilions and other expenses?

It is evident that our participation should be more modest. What we can sell must be advertised more effectively. It is not a matter of prestige only.

Mikhailov, Smolensk.

IN my opinion it's high time to radically reconsider the principles and methods of our foreign trade and work out new concepts of our foreign economic policy. The necessity of this step is evident not just inside but outside, which becomes clear from the interview given by Eric Schmidt, director of the European Institute for Foreign Trade. At the market of European countries Soviet export is limited to fuel and raw materials, which is humiliating for such a great power. It's hard to admit but Mr Schmidt has truly estimated the gist of foreign trade: 'You are selling your raw materials on the world market for deplorably low prices.'

Indeed in the past twenty years we have poured out upon the markets of European countries over two billion tons of oil and oil products. And how did we use the money which we got for the sale of oil? The sum amounted to R200–250 billion. Look around and see. The deplorable state of our economy will give you an answer. As a specialist in the field of foreign relations I share the opinion of Mr Schmidt that we shouldn't set goals which can't be achieved.

And, as for looking for partners among big Western concerns, it would be more realistic to look for them among developing countries. In my opinion this is a very important viewpoint on our foreign trade orientation. I am inclined to think that so far we have been attaching too much importance to the political aspects of the problem. It is for you to judge. Our foreign trade with socialist countries amounted to two-thirds of total turnover. Our trade with industrialized capitalist countries counted for one-quarter and our trade with developing countries 1 per cent. What is more, the bulk of our foreign trade was with five main countries: East Germany, Czechoslovakia, Poland, Bulgaria and Hungary.

This narrow specialization of our foreign economic relationship is fraught with very serious problems. In spite of the fact that the Soviet Union maintains trade and economic relations with 140 countries of the world, we actively trade with only twenty countries. Five countries belong to the Council for Mutual Economic Assistance, eleven countries are capitalist and four countries are developing. The total share is 70 per cent of foreign trade turnover. I believe that the principles of our foreign trade orientation should be reconsidered. Our partners among developing countries which are rapidly gaining their economic and export potential and can offer a wide range of high-quality consumer goods as well as markets for Soviet exports deserve closer attention.

Gorshkov, an economist, Moscow.

THERE is no secret that our industry and agriculture cannot supply our population with all the necessary goods. But is the deficit always justified? According to the newspaper *Trud* of 15 April, during the inspection of the trust Kharkov Fish the workers' inspectors discovered more than R300 million worth of hidden products. And in the city it is impossible to buy any fish. There are queues for everything.

The newspaper *Kazakhstan Pravda*, dated 18 April, said over

150,000 boxes of detergent, 145,000 tons of soap, lots of toothpaste, shampoo and other things were discovered at the Taldeturgan base. And mothers have to stand for hours in queues to get a cake of soap or a box of detergent. What is this, open sabotage? And how are those responsible for this punished? Well, someone is expelled from the trade union, another gets a reprimand.

One mustn't forget that this part of our society, this category of people, is often connected with mafias and they have in their hands political, social and economic strings. They purposely create hardships in the life of our people and they undermine the authority of our society in the international arena. Let them think that socialism cannot supply the population even with soap.

While I'm writing these lines, the Kazakh radio reports great deposits of deficit have been discovered in the city of Saran. There were dozens of officials of various ranks from People's Control, including the chairman of the executive committee of the city, and it was only thanks to the interference of the regional party committee that it became possible to start an investigation. Judging by the Press reports, this is a widespread epidemic. Hundreds of millions of roubles as a result are excluded from the turnover. They want our people to believe that perestroika is to blame for what is going on. Practice shows that the existing committees of the People's Control don't cope with their obligations. What's more they often defend all kinds of crooks.

Brezhgalin, Timertao.

WHEN I was on a business trip to France I had a chance to compare the earnings and prices there and in this country. As a result of the comparison I came to the conclusion that our Soviet rouble was equivalent, approximately, to ten francs. The rate of exchange for French tourists going to the USSR is one franc to one rouble. Who made this robbery of our poor country lawful? It's a State crime. I'll give one example. A worker in our country earns a maximum of R500–600 a month. When he goes to France he will exchange R500 for 500 francs. With this money our Soviet tourist can have dinner twice. Or he can buy half a camera, Kiev type. In

France such a camera costs 1,000 francs. A French worker gets a minimum of 5,000 francs. Coming to our country he can exchange them for R5,000. With these he can buy fifty cameras at the price of R100. In whose interest is all this?

Murasev, City of Nhezhetaget.

SOME people believe that the only way of preventing the collapse of the consumer market is currency reform. But will it help? One of the main causes of this situation is that people concerned about the purchasing power of the rouble are trying to spend their money. This stimulates the growth of prices which in turn further decreases the purchasing power of the rouble. A chain reaction happens. Communists call it a run of money and it threatens to undermine our economy totally. Can a currency reform help in such a situation? I hardly think so. All the talk of reform only makes the situation worse.

One can understand the behaviour of the people. What's the point of keeping money, the value of which is rapidly falling? To check this process we need to make people interested in keeping the cash in their money boxes. I suggest the following: since each note has its own number it will be possible to arrange lotteries. The owners of lucky numbers will win prizes. It could be quite cheap for the government. The prizes could be a coupon to buy commodities which are in short supply. Big notes should be used for this purpose, of course. Then it might be possible not to resort to such a measure as currency reform.

Shwetzer, an economist.

WITH all the differences of opinion among economists today, there is still one holy cow which for some reason no one dare touch – and that is the five-year plan. Of course the current five-year plan is coming in for some fairly severe criticism, some of it on the pages of *AIF*, but for some reason no one has any doubt that in its wake there will be another plan, and a five-year one at that.

I would like to put forward a suggestion, which is that this new plan may well turn out to be counter-productive in the process of restructuring the economic mechanism, just like the present one is. The problem is not one of the quality of the plan itself, but of the timescale.

It may well be that five years is a sensible period in the life of a stable, smoothly functioning economy, but in a period of restructuring or perestroika, it is far too long. We have still not reached agreement on what sort of economy it will be, and it is fairly obvious that there will be all sorts of unexpected side-effects from the process of change, and that we will have to take measures to regulate all the imbalances that crop up as we go along, as we try to 'run in' our new economic system.

In this situation, the five-year plan – if indeed we are going to stick with it – will shackle the hands of the economic leaders, and if we are not necessarily going to stick to it, then why do we need it at all? In other words, the basic concepts of the five-year plan cannot help but get out of date during its lifetime. Would it not be better during the changeover period to limit ourselves to operational planning, and to draw up plans for no more than two or three years at a time? Not to mention the fact that not only the actual figures but even the very status of the plan could undergo cardinal changes in this period of self-regulation (although, of course, as far as I am aware no civilized country can ever totally abandon planning).

Yu Rybalov, economist, Novosibirsk.

WHY is it that everyone in the Soviet Union is out to get what he wants while there isn't enough to go round? The local councils are after authority, the party's upper crust are clinging to their privileges, the miners and tractor drivers are campaigning for benefits. The list could go on and on. There is much talk about the need for a market-based economy which will put everything to rights, and once again someone is suggesting price hikes.

It would do us good to turn to history for a moment. Reforms were only successful when they were intended to change the situation of the working people, of every individual worker, farmer or public servant. When it comes to markets, I give my full support to the idea of a labour market. Every person who is employed and is therefore beneficial to society should be able to sell his labour to whomever wants to buy it, a State-owned enterprise, a collective farm or a private individual.

There should be a framework within which ordinary people like myself can offer their services and have something offered in exchange and decide for themselves whether or not they want to sell their work at whatever price. I can envisage a situation where I will want to minimize my plant's indirect overheads and where I will want to know what percentage of my wages goes on unnecessary paperwork. This should be the axis of the policy of perestroika. We are all sick to death of parliamentary debate and discussions in the Press. Parliament and the Press are busy dealing with the issues that interest them, while our living standards are going downhill.

And now we are being threatened with an overall prices hike, despite already inflated prices, and there are people counting other people's money and making no allowances for how people have earned their incomes.

The advent of co-operatives has turned employees of enterprises into the lowest income group. Barrack-room socialism must be wiped out at enterprises, collective farms, State farms, in fact everywhere, the way serfdom was abolished by the Tsar in 1861. That reform set Russia on the road to capitalism, a more progressive social system. All other legislative acts were or were not passed depending on how they fitted into the abolition of serfdom. That is precisely the way things should be done today. If the worker gets the chance to sell his labour, all other laws must back him and then things will take care of themselves, and all working people will become willing contributors to perestroika at the workplace. They will do so because the thickness of their wallets will directly depend upon the success of perestroika, and perestroika will finally reach all levels from local to Union Republics, and national.

A. Ryabov, Zagorsk, Moscow region.

ALMOST every day sees television and newspaper reports about freight trains waiting to be unloaded. It is a Catch-22 situation that will not change until we start making culprits responsible. Fines for freight train idle time are imposed on organizations rather than on those who caused it. Is there any point in them?

The government should have thought better than to increase the fines by 400 per cent. This will not lead anywhere. The people who are responsible for idle time should be fined or taken to court.

K. Domozhirov, Voronovo, Tomsk region.

I would like to share my indignation about the new Supreme Soviet decree 'On Taxation of the Labour Remuneration Fund'. As a result of this decree cost-accounting teams are left with R3,000 between ten people after paying all taxes, and the following month are left with R4,000 only if they economize on resources and raise productivity. But the team actually gets only R3,250, because R750 goes to the State in taxation. It's nothing more than robbery pure and simple! What other countries make people pay three times as much tax as they earn? Of course, an exception has been made for the producers of consumer goods. This means that workers in the steel industry, for example, are being penalized because they produce steel and not the final consumer products like irons.

At one point the decree says '... regardless of which form of cost-accounting is used ...', thereby including leasing brigades as well. The whole idea behind leasing is that you supposedly have the right to all of your income; however, this taxation law nips that one in the bud.

I was very disappointed in Academician Abalkin for drawing up this decree, and in the Supreme Soviet for not grasping what effect it would have and for letting it go through. Like many decrees before, it reaches deep into the pockets of those who can least afford to pay, and lets the co-operatives and the black economy right off. This sort of tax legislation takes away any incentive to work at all, and doesn't encourage people to think about saving resources. It does nothing to encourage increased productivity, in fact it does the reverse, which means that the situation in the country will deteriorate.

G. Smolensky, worker, 'Zapstroitrans', Leningrad.

AT the end of January the USSR State Statistics Committee published statistics relating to the socio-economic development of the country in 1989. These statistics show growth in almost all areas of the economy, including the standard of living indices (salaries, etc.).

However, this growth does not show the real state of affairs since it takes no account of inflation. By not making adjustment for inflation the Soviet Union's main statistics office has kept the real level of inflation a secret. According to its information, inflation was 7.5 per cent in 1989. But in calculating this figure they haven't taken into account higher prices on consumer goods and services or the lower (at very best, same as before) quality of these goods and services. At the same time, according to figures issued by Gosplan's* Economic Research Institute, the rise in inflation taking into account this factor alone is 11 per cent. It is simply not possible to ignore it.

That is why I think that the real level of inflation in 1989 was nearer the 16.5 per cent mark (11 per cent price increases, 5.5 per cent unsatisfied consumer demand for goods and services). If we take into account the real level of inflation, all the standard of living indices for 1989 have fallen considerably when compared with 1988, and not the reverse, as is claimed by the USSR State Statistics Committee.

If we carry on at this rate, in three to four years' time the Soviet rouble will be worth half of what it is now.

Inflation is not only eating into, indeed eating up, all our efforts to increase the material welfare of the population, but also eating into those areas that were more or less all right before. In other words, the basis that already existed in 1989 for improving the standard of living has not been used due to excessive inflation. The standard of living has also fallen because we still do not have a proper system for protecting people; there are no State measures to protect the standard of living we have already reached.

Does our government worry about this? Yes it does, and as a result it intends to introduce a cost of living index by 1997. Wonderful. That means we only have to be patient for another six or seven years . . .

A. Gorshkov, candidate of economic sciences.

* Gosplan is the USSR State Planning Committee.

THE newspaper *Moscow Pravda* recently published data from the control and revision commission of the Moscow City organization of the CPSU on the damage and plunder of equipment on which twenty-eight million convertible roubles had been spent. Those who were to blame received only reprimands. Recently the TV programme *Six Hundred Seconds* highlighted the case of a worker who stole from his factory coffee worth R200. She was imprisoned for six years. What does it mean when people with party cards are not under the jurisdiction of the courts?

L. S. Lubertsi, Moscow.

OUR Toganrok combine was divided into four separate plants and now each one has its own director, its own management, party committee, young communist league committee, trade union committee and personnel department. And each director has several deputies, chief specialists, with their deputies and staffs. All this is called the amalgamated production, at the head of which is a general director, with his deputies, his chief engineers and their deputies, chief specialists and their deputies and with a full staff of employees with party committee, young communist league committee, union committee and staff department.

However, the actual number of workers became lower. Where does the information come from that the numbers employed in management in our country has declined? Or could it be that there are many places where there are no directors at the head of plants?

A. Zolitscoya, Toganrok.

THE State deficit is estimated now at over R100 billion. It has considerably increased as a result of strikes, especially in the mines. Those who are responsible for them should pay the damages, at least partially. Of course, I don't put the blame on the strikers. They stopped working because they could see no other way out of the situation. It all happened through the fault of the management and the party and trade union leaders. It will be a warning to others. If your methods

140

of management are to the detriment of the country you should be held responsible.

Alexandrov, Moscow.

COULD you take a look and see whether Mr Ryzhkov and his minister wear socks. If they do, could you ask them where they buy them?

E. R. Dnepropetrovsk region.

(*A variation on the shortage joke. One going the rounds recently was: Yeltsin has a new economic plan, a two-day one. On day one he'll declare war on Sweden, And on day two . . . ? Surrender, of course – Ed.*)

I want to correct one of the great extremes of perestroika – and build new breweries. To do that we will have to form a new party, Alcoholics of the USSR. It's sure to be the biggest party in the world. The entrance fee will be in goods – three cases of empty bottles or one case of full bottles.

V. S., Moscow.

*   *   *

STATE and collective farms in Volgagrad province have begun to plan their crops for the last year of the present five-year plan. It seems unbelievable, but they have actually decided to cut their production of vegetables, i.e. sowing and planting, by half. It turns out that last year, only 50 per cent of vegetables were harvested. The rest were ploughed back into the soil. Last year, you could buy tomato juice at every street stall, all year round. This year, there has been none. Even the advertisement, advocating the goodness of tomato juice, has disappeared. Other tomato products, such as tomato purée, are no longer available in shops.

During the tomato season, urban dwellers found themselves in endless queues in the hope of buying tomatoes. Then came the explanation: tomatoes had joined the list of food products for intensive food processing, and large quantities of them were being sent to factories to be put into tins and tubes. In fact what was happening was that they were being intensively ploughed back into the soil. When this became known, they popped up with a new explanation: shortage of labour and transport difficulties.

Other vegetables, such as cabbage, shared the fate of the tomato. Fifty per cent of ready-to-eat cabbage was ploughed back into the soil. Yet we all know the story of Astrakhan water melons. When the melon growers of Astrakhan realized that they had a glut of ripe water melons, they started giving them away, free, to anyone who would pick them. When the authorities found out, any problems with labour, transport or storage disappeared, as if by magic. Pity that the Volgagrad vegetable growers have not thought of doing the same. Wasting good food is a crime.

V. Senko, Volgagrad.

(*The Soviet Union has something like three and a half million agricultural supervisors whose hands never touch the earth: the USA has two and a quarter million farmers who feed the country, and then some – Ed.*)

WE have been inventing, looking with closed eyes for many, many years and we have been experimenting in the field of agriculture. But there is an open door in front of us and we are trying to come in through the window. In nature, despite the social structure, there is only one law of development. The formulae of Einstein are used by all scientists of the world and nobody says that those formulae are capitalistic.

Or for example, let's take aerodynamics. No one will accuse us that our Buryan is very close, almost like a twin brother of the Shuttle. It could not be otherwise, because the physical laws are the same for everybody. Submarines, rockets, aircraft and so on are being designed in accordance with the same rules. So where on earth did the idea come from that in the socialist way of development there should be something in it different to the development of capitalistic society? It's high time we gave up dogmatism and started to study attentively and carefully the progressive experience of the developed countries in the field of agriculture. It's high time we became brave enough to apply it in our country.

V. Zhemirenka, Kharkov.

WE hear all the time that our country is vast and its resources are enormous, yet why are we so poor? It's because no one is responsible for the richness we have. There is not even a reasonable payment for the use of the most important State asset, land. Rent from State farms and collective farms and from peasant land is the only source of richness both for the State and the peasant. Experts say that the land in use is more than 550 million hectares and with the average rather modest rent payment per hectare of say R200 per hectare we could have about R100 billion as rent payment. This would cover the State's budget deficit and would help iron out economic imbalances.

We have to, as soon as possible, work out the valuation of the land and introduce a differential payment system for its use in different areas of the agricultural economy. The State and collective farms will have to give up excess land: they will work more efficiently on smaller lands. Thus the land gain can also be distributed to peasants on rental terms.

V. Samarin.

THE fruit-picking season begins soon in Astrakhan region. Everything is plentiful: apricots, cherries – and if you don't have them in your garden it's easy to buy them at the bazaar for three or four roubles a bucket. In gardens there are apples, pears, peaches, strawberries and so on. But we can't make preserves for the winter because we get only 1.5 kilos of sugar a month per person and for the military families only 1 kilo. In a shop I saw a three-litre tank of compote of berries for five roubles. But it would have only cost me forty to fifty kopecks to make myself. Of course a ten times price difference is very noticeable in the family budget.

Apart from all this, how are we going to participate in the implementation of the food programme? We're even going to deplete it because in the autumn we have to go to the shops to buy jams, juice and other things. It's also very difficult to find these items in our stores. If there is a coupon system then it should work efficiently and rationed items should be available. Today it's the 24th and for the last month I haven't been able to get sugar.

N. Davidova, Astrakhan region.

IT'S been said that perestroika will only begin in the minds of our people when the food problem is solved. That's absolutely right. It's the most important issue in our struggle for socialism, for peace, for life itself. During the war the workers who were involved in the manufacturing of military products were not called up into the Soviet army but remained in the cities. We should use the same system now for young boys working in agriculture until such time as we solve the food problem.

I don't think that this extraordinary step will harm our defence but by this we can give rebirth to our village. It can be filled with technical facilities, with different investments, we can make the soil fertile – but there are no young people interested in the work, there are no strong young families in the village and without this the village will remain dead, deaf to all initiatives. By sending our sons from the village to the army, as a rule, we lose them for ever. Girls waiting on the men also leave the village. And the younger brothers seeing the example of their elder brothers and sisters also leave.

There are no strong young people remaining. We say that it's high time the country paid back its debt to the villages, but let us at least keep our sons and daughters in them as cities are taking them away. Apart from that, who is our army going to defend when our villages and agriculture are a complete ruin?

A. Tchupashkin, Moscow.

THERE is a shortage of labour in agriculture. I and others want to work in agriculture but to do that an urgent problem has to be solved, the provision of decent living conditions in villages. For working long-term in the mines I got a four-room flat, well equipped. Now my six children have left home and there is only me and my wife. I was entitled to a pension at the age of fifty-two but I'm strong enough still to work and

I want to continue to work in a rural area. But there is no place to live. To buy a house costs too much for me. It wasn't possible for me to save money with such a big family as mine.

I have contributed a lot in the mines to get the flat I have now. But nowadays I do not bring any profit to my mine because the enterprise needs young people to work. I propose this: that the mine buys me a house in a rural area and as an obligatory condition I give to it my city flat. By doing this the mine can improve the working condition for someone who is working there and it would also benefit the State. Because if I was living in the country I could be producing in my own garden and also working on a collective farm.

A. Pianov, Severia, Uralsk.

I am entitled to a pension but I am still working. I have four cows, eleven bull calves, twenty-three sheep, two pigs and last year provided to the State three tons, 300 kilograms of meat. The year before that four tons of meat. I bred and sold thirteen cows and in the last three months I provided 1,500 litres of milk to the State. My family, which consists of fifteen people, is self-sufficient in meat and milk – however I lack certain things to maintain all this. I only have 800 square metres of land and on this I have my house and farm buildings. I have written several times to the chairman of the rural Soviet with the request that they provide me with an additional piece of land. The reply was 'we don't have any land' and several other things it wouldn't be helpful to quote in the interest of perestroika.

Because I couldn't get any more land I had to kill with an axe nineteen hens as it was impossible to let them out. I asked the city council for land but the response I got from the deputy chairman was 'go to the USA, you'll get land there.'

L. Shilova, Moscow region.

THE foreign trade organization employees of our country speak a lot about the importing of various foodstuffs and almost nothing about exporting. Maybe they mean that our exports are negligible and discussion about it is pointless.

Maybe our newspapers too have been hypnotized by the foreign trade officials. But I want to be brave enough to confirm quite the opposite. It's true that our foodstuff exports hardly compare with imports. But nevertheless we sell abroad annually more than two billion kilograms of the main products, excluding grain, and we get approximately R500 million.

What makes up the exports? Excluding perishables which amount to several million kilos, we also export flour and cereals (600m. km.), sugar (150–200m. km.), vegetable oil (120m. km.), vegetables and fruit (50m. km.), meat and meat products (300–340m. km.), cans of meat (80,000 tins), honey (20m. km.), butter (20m. km.), milk products (60m. km.). What is the geography of our food exports? Approximately half of the products we supply to the socialist bloc countries, then to Cuba and Vietnam, then a quarter goes to the developing countries and we also export to the developed capitalist countries: annually we sent about 500 million kilos of high-quality products.

But what does two billion kilograms mean for a country that nowadays has a rationing system? It's not difficult to estimate, taking into account the rationing system, how many citizens of our country we could provide for from these exported goods. From flour and cereals 50–60 million people; sugar 15–20 million; oil 12–20 million; honey 20–30 million; butter $1\frac{1}{2}$–2 million; meat and meat products $1\frac{1}{2}$–2 million; vegetables and fruit 1–2 million people.

A. Garshkov, candidate of economics.

THE seminar on food problems in Kharkov which was shown on TV aroused both interest and indignation. On the screen you could see milk and meat products in great variety. Even in the years of abundance when one could buy sausage at the price of R2.60 a kilogram, butter, cheese and condensed milk, I saw nothing like this. What I can't understand is for whom this show was meant. Who do we want to deceive? Why didn't the organizers of this seminar ask the common people of Kharkov whether there was butter and cheese on sale? As for potatoes, they cost R1.30 at the markets because there are no potatoes on sale in the shops. What are we to do; I mean those old age pensioners who get fifty or seventy roubles a month?

L. Savein, pensioner, Kharkov.

ACCORDING to the radio a big load of water melons was brought to Kamchatka from Uzbekistan but they were thrown away because they had got spoiled. Such was the case with onions, potatoes and citrus fruits. Allegedly the produce was handed over to the Committee of People's Control. The newspaper *Izvestia* gave facts about the loss of R1.8 billion worth of leather and those who were responsible for that were just told to improve the situation within a year.

The Committee of People's Control also started the machinations at the tobacco factory Yava. They were hiding eight million boxes of cigarettes. Those responsible were punished. They got reprimands. What is going on? Is it an open sabotage? What measures are taken against all this? This is just encouraging things. There are many examples like these. If the crimes are not punished perestroika will make no progress.

M. Tchitvirkina, Rostov on the Don.

WE live in a Byelorussian village. Is it profitable for an individual to raise a pig? Well, here are the facts. In order to raise a pig weighing 150 kilograms, one and a half tons of potatoes are needed. One kilogram of potatoes costs twenty kopecks. One and a half tons costs R300. Besides that you have to pay sixty roubles for a pig at the market. So it will cost you R360, to say nothing of the labour involved.

The State purchasing price for one kilogram of pork is R2.10. So the peasant gets R315. Thus the net loss is forty-five roubles.

Well, can anyone expect an increase in the production of meat from individuals? Isn't it better to sell potatoes and with the money saved go to the regional centre and buy meat at the price of two roubles a kilo? The difference is that instead of producing food products, the peasant becomes a consumer.

Gerasemchek, Grodnin region.

I live not far from the State farm Sloganski. Last autumn, because of the shortage of petrol, the lorries and machines were at a standstill. The fields had been ploughed and they were red with tomatoes but the harvest was not reaped. The shops are empty. There are no tomatoes, no tomato paste, to say nothing of tomato juice. Yesterday on TV they showed a pipeline from the USSR to Iran. Well, isn't it better to use that oil for our own needs so that we could have tomatoes and other vegetables?

Just the same, the common people don't see any imported goods on sale. I have the impression that soon we ourselves will be sold. It's impossible to buy a sheet of paper.

Siverenko, City of Slogansk.

WHEN contenders for ministerial posts were appointed by a recent session of the Supreme Soviet, the new chairman of the USSR State Committee for Statistics promised that his organization would not lie to the public any more. I doubt his sincerity. The problem is that in order to stop deceiving the public all the statistical data that has been accumulated over the past seven decades would have to be pronounced invalid. I would like to illustrate my point.

I have in my hands a book entitled *USSR Economy in 1973*. I will now cite several figures, and if I don't hear any laughter through tears I will know that either you do not have a sense of humour or that you are not patriotic.

So, in 1916 Russia had 58.4 million head of cattle, including 28.8 million cows, and it produced 1.9 million tons of beef, 366,000 tons of vegetable oil and 29.4 million tons of milk.

In 1973, the Soviet Union had 106.3 million head of cattle, including 41.9 million cows producing 5.9 million tons of beef (three times as much as in 1916), 1.35 million tons of vegetable oil (four times as much) and 88.3 million tons of milk (three times as much)!

I wonder how this country could have produced 200 per cent more milk by increasing the number of cows by only 50 per cent, while it is public knowledge that our milk yield per cow cannot possibly be lower?

Since 1973, Soviet output statistics for meat, milk and other products have grown astronomically. But the shelves in the shops are empty enough to make anyone speechless with fury and despair.

I hereby state that all statistics books published in this country since 1917 are full of lies, and that now, in the day of the so-called glasnost, the authorities are scared to publish the true figures indicating how much 'progress' we have made as a country.

This will have to be done, sooner or later. They ought to act as befits men.

A. Obrastsov, Leningrad.

MR Ligachev, then Secretary of the CPSU Central Committee, told the second Congress of People's Deputies that the USSR's annual meat production was 66 kg. per capita. Later Gorbachev stated that in 1989 the USSR had produced 11.4 million tons of meat. Divided between the 280 million population, this figure goes down to 40 kg. per capita. Leaving out the bones (at least 50 per cent of the weight) and fat (25 per cent), our estimation of per capita meat consumption in the Soviet Union comes down to 15 kg. a year, or about 1 kg. a month.

P. Shirokhov, Tallinn.

LIFE for us was not very enjoyable. We didn't have an apartment, my wife and I both worked at the factory for a pittance and could barely make ends meet. The future didn't look any better either. Then the times changed. We both left the factory and set up a co-operative. We bought a small piece of land and went into horticulture. Suddenly we were very busy with hardly any spare time, in the summer selling our flowers and in winter selling kebabs.

People say that there is no meat in the country, but that's not true, there's plenty of meat, I buy whole sides of it in the local shops, and if I can't get it there, I go to the meat processing factory where it's always available. They say there's no sugar either, but don't you believe it. I personally sell sacks of it to illegal alcohol distillers. You can get anything in the Soviet Union, you just have to know where to go. Before I was a nobody. Now everyone knows me from the doctors to the bosses and the militia.

I saw my daughter married and bought her a co-operative apartment and a car. Now I've got my own dacha, a four-room apartment and a Volga car. The next thing I'm going to do is to buy my son a car, I want him to have everything. Before I used to have to tug my forelock to everyone – now it's the other way round. I would like to spit in the face of anyone who does not believe in perestroika. I know it works. I would like to thank the party, the government and Mr Gorbachev personally for helping us. It is thanks to them that we have been able to start living like human beings. Long may it last.

Yours respectfully, A. Abramov, Achinsk, Krasnoyarsk district.

I learned from the programme *Time* about our aid to the fraternal Rumanian people. It made me indignant. I was not indignant about the fact that we are rendering fraternal aid but I was indignant because we are sending sugar and buckwheat. Well, we can get sugar on coupons, but as far as buckwheat is concerned our family has forgotten the taste. And my little grandchildren don't even know what it is. In our republic buckwheat is prescribed by doctors only to diabetics. Our people have to eat barley and both children and grown-ups are sick and tired of it. There is a great shortage of products and I am angry that we are giving away our goods to others while we experience such a great deficit in everything. Why is it being done on behalf of our people and behind the backs of our people? Such a policy is not in the interests of the common people.

Pashan, City of Tiraspol.

FOLK wisdom has it that the one who saves is wiser than the one who is rich. Indeed, our harvests are no guarantee that people will have enough to eat till next autumn. Everybody knows why: we lose too much because of our carelessness. Any sane person will find it hard to believe that we lose almost as much grain as we buy in from other countries in exchange for our non-renewable resources such as oil, gas and iron ore. Moreover, in 1984 one ton of oil could buy four tons of grain, whereas last year one ton of oil could buy only 1.5 tons of grain. At the same time a quarter of our grain harvest is lost.

According to information gathered by the State Committee for Statistics in 131 cities in May of this year, meat was not on sale in a third of these cities and beef and pork could not be bought in every other city; frankfurters and smoked sausages were absent in 75–80 per cent of the cities under survey and cheese and cream in 35 per cent.

On average, during the first six months of this year the State-run retail trade and catering establishments in eighteen regions of the country sold less than one kilogram of meat and poultry a month per capita and in more than twenty regions less than 300 grams of butter.

At the same time 500 railway cars loaded with meat products stood unattended for a week at Moscow railway station. As a result of such mismanagement, one million tons of meat products are lost each year.

At the peak of the harvesting season mountains of vegetables and fruit are perishing because of bad roads and a shortage of railway cars, refrigeration and storage facilities and also due to carelessness of officials responsible for delivery and supply.

As another old saying goes, 'Disorder may destroy a strong army.' What, then, is to be done? The best solution is to make the producer the owner and manager of his own produce.

A. F.

Question and Answer

HOW many loss-making enterprises are there in the Soviet Union and what are we going to do about them?

Yu Kochnov, Tula.

Candidate of Economics, A. Stoinik, of the USSR Academy of Sciences' Institute of Economics, answers:

Loss-making enterprises are one of the things we have

inherited from the old command-administrative system of management. Central planning prices, expenditure, objectives, distribution of resources, funds, transfer of funds from profitable to non-profit-making enterprises – all this conspired against the enterprises trying to take a direct interest in working more efficiently or economizing on resources, and made them feel as if nothing depended on themselves.

Unfortunately Soviet law has laid down the exact definition of loss-making. This means that we are still left with what are called 'planned loss-makers', which exist on State subsidies.

At the present time we have about 24,000 loss-making enterprises in the Soviet Union, making between them a loss of around R11 billion. According to the USSR State Statistics Committee, in 1987 one in seven industrial enterprises were loss-makers, and these losses totalled R4.3 billion.

There are plenty of them in other sectors too: in the fuel and energy industry one in six are unprofitable, in the coal industry one in five and in the service sector one quarter turn in regular losses.

The Soviet Union's construction industry is also a regular loss-maker. Every year the State pours roughly 37 per cent of its budget into capital construction projects, and these resources are used inefficiently. Construction enterprises lag permanently 250 to 300 per cent behind demand. It takes them 2.7 times as long to complete construction projects as planned, and they only put an average of twelve construction workers on to each project. There are over R9 billion frozen in incompleted building projects all over the country, with R14.2 billion worth of equipment standing idle.

The agricultural industry is no better off with one in six enterprises (total 6,500) making losses. Despite a huge State subsidy of R87 billion to the agricultural industry, we still have to buy quite a lot of food abroad.

With the new economic reforms that are coming in, we can no longer afford to keep the old loss-makers running. Although the new Law on State Enterprises does define the means for dealing with this economic problem, it cannot be said that any of the ministries have shown any interest in doing anything about it over the last three years. The ministries have continued to receive their allowances from the State budget and contributions from profitable enterprises to industry funds and have continued to grant-aid non-profitable enterprises or to append them administratively to profitable outfits, which, incidentally, is in contravention of the Law on State Enterprises. It is obvious that without the support of the workers themselves we cannot solve this problem.

One way out is the leasing contract. The Butovsk construction materials combine in Moscow district was one of the pioneers in this scheme. In 1987 the State was subsidizing this combine to the tune of R70,000. However, in the first ten months of 1988 alone they turned in a profit of R800,000. At the same time their salaries went up by 25 per cent and their productivity by 30 per cent. Another 500 enterprises of varying different sorts in the Moscow district have now followed their example.

These good figures are the result of successfully combining a leasing contract and attracting private capital in the form of a share issue to the employees. The Lvov 'Konveyor' combine and the 'Arsenovsky' State farm in Kemerovo, and the 'Zavety Lenina' State farm in Moscow district have also now become joint-stock companies.

Leasing and other forms of contract are proving to be the most reliable and practical way of turning round loss-making enterprises in the agricultural sector. Within a short time production can go up by 20–30 per cent, and productivity by a factor of 1.5 to 2.

Finally, of course, the least painful way of getting rid of loss-making enterprises, units, farms, etc. is by transferring them to co-operative ownership. Take for example the 'Mayak' co-operative, set up under the Bryansk factory which produces large-scale panels. As soon as it started work its output increased one and a half times and the unit started bringing in profits, out of which the workers paid themselves higher salaries.

WHY is it that in the 'country of birch-coloured cotton' it has become difficult, if not impossible, to acquire good-quality fabrics made from natural fibres, or clothes made from them?

O. Erofeeva, Smolensk district.

I. Ustinov, candidate of economic sciences, answers:

In recent years the rate of fabric production has obviously slowed down, if not stagnated. Meanwhile, exports are considerably up and imports down. There can be no justification for such a situation. In 1989 the USSR exported 539.7 million metres of fabric, i.e. 3.5 times as much as it did in 1985. As a result, given that the population has increased during that period, the average per capita consumption of fabric has fallen.

Over the last five-year period alone fabric production in the USSR has risen by a factor of 1.1 only, while sales abroad are three and a half times the figure at the beginning of this period. At the same time purchases have fallen by a factor of more than two. We have managed to destabilize our domestic textile market.

Whereas five years ago we were importing almost 420 million metres more fabric than we exported, last year we were exporting 212 million metres more than we were buying abroad.

To be objective we must point out that until 1985 the Soviet fabric export market was stagnating. It was after 1985 that the present unexpected export boom started, which meant that during one five-year period alone we sent 3.5 times more fabric abroad, including almost four times as much pure cotton, seven times as much linen and more than two and a half times as much wool.

Fabric trading is very much to our disadvantage. In exchange for the 442 million metres of pure cotton fabrics it sold last year, the Soviet Union received approximately R170 million, which works out at an average of 38 kopecks per metre. During the same year we bought roughly 189 million metres of cotton fabrics abroad at a cost of R247 million, or 1.31 per metre.

Last year alone the USSR exported 253 million metres more of these fabrics than it bought abroad, but made a loss of R77 million on the exchange.

The 'price scissors' of fabric import/export, and not only fabric, has not lessened over recent times, but enlarged, and not to our advantage. Whereas in 1980 we had to sell 2.7 metres of Soviet-produced fabric in order to buy in 1 metre of foreign cloth, last year we found that this had risen to 3.4

metres of Soviet fabric at a conservative calculation. How can we possibly explain, let alone justify, continuing to trade in this way?

This is the background behind the paucity of the Soviet market, prices going berserk and leap-frogging shortages.

Over the last five years the Soviet Union has produced 6.6 million fewer cotton suits, and 16.8 million fewer cotton trousers than ever before. The story is the same for other items of clothing.

In 1989 alone the USSR bought in from abroad R3.2 billion worth of clothing and underwear, which is almost 4.5 as much as it did in 1970. At the same time we have spent only R1.4 billion on buying equipment for the clothing industry in the last twenty years, in other words 4 per cent of the amount spent on purchasing foreign-made clothing and underwear. And all this against a background of falling production of domestically produced equipment for clothing manufacture.

Soviet fabric exports (millions metres)

	Total	Cotton	Linen	Wool	Silk & Staple
1980	172.6	123.6	2.3	1.7	45.0
1985	153.0	116.5	1.9	4.1	30.5
1986	208.7	163.0	9.7	4.4	31.6
1987	388.7	311.8	15.9	3.8	57.2
1988	458.1	376.1	20.6	7.9	53.5
1989	539.7	441.8	25.6	8.3	64.0
Total					
1980–84	652.6	448.3	10.7	11.2	182.4
1985–89	1,711.2	1,372.5	73.7	28.6	236.4

It is high time to stop financing the light industry of neighbouring countries. The first step in this direction should be to reduce by one third the export of home-produced fabrics, and to stop using the majority of foreign currency earnings to buy new clothes from abroad, but to use them instead for buying modern clothing factories, if at all possible as turnkey projects.

I read recently in the magazine *Communist* that the USSR's foreign debts stood at more than R40 billion. But how much is owed to the Soviet Union and who are our largest debtors?

A. Burenin, Moscow.

The USSR Ministry of Finance put the figures for 1 November 1989 at R85.8 billion. Debt repayments are expected to be in the region of R17.2 billion in 1990. The USSR plans to give free aid to foreign countries this year of approximately R1.6 billion. The following countries rate as some of our largest debtors.

(In million roubles)

Cuba	154,906
Vietnam	91,312
Syria	67,426
Iraq	37,426
Ethiopia	28,605
Korea	22,341
Mongolia	95,427
India	89,075
Poland	4,955
Afghanistan	3,055
Algeria	25,193
Angola	20,289

WHY have ladies' tights, the choice of which was extremely narrow previously, disappeared altogether? The ones on sale are made by co-operatives and are extremely expensive. Have hosiery factories been closed down?

G. J., Moscow.

'No. All the factories are working normally,' says R. Kuznetsova, manager of Moscow's Tushino hosiery factory. 'Despite difficulties we produce twenty million pairs of ladies' and five million pairs of children's tights annually. But this is not much for a city with four million women – and visitors. But we physically cannot increase our output because our premises were built more than a hundred years ago and it is impossible to enlarge our building.'

Deputy head of the Department of Knit-wear Industry of the USSR Ministry of Light Industry, Y. Papiyan, says: 'Soviet factories produce 240 million pairs of ladies' tights annually and next year the production will increase to 400 million. We've bought equipment in Japan and Italy which is arriving already and factories will be located throughout the country.'

This will work out at three pairs of tights a year for every woman. How many are actually needed?

'At least six,' says marketing expert of the USSR Ministry of Trade A. Gulyayeva, 'if we stick to the old practice of buying a pair of tights to last. In the West tights are a disposable item. The US, with a smaller population, produces 1.5 billion annually.'

WE had a good harvest of garlic this year. I applied to the local consumer co-operatives' society but it refused to buy my garlic. Over 100 people had the same trouble in our village alone. Imagine how many there were in the entire region and republic.

As a result I had to dump 500 kilos of this year's garlic. Is it easier and cheaper to purchase garlic abroad, as we do at present?

Yavgeny Filatov, deputy head of the vegetables supplies department of the Central Consumers Co-operatives Society, replies:

This year the USSR Committee for Agriculture purchased a large quantity of garlic from China and Vietnam. Possibilities for home production were not taken into account. Annual purchases of garlic were formerly meant for Siberia and the Far East, though to date Chinese and Vietnamese garlic has been supplied to more western areas – up to the Ukraine. With sufficient garlic on the home market, purchase from domestic producers has been suspended.

HOW do we measure how much meat we eat per capita in the Soviet Union, and is this different in the various republics?

V. Ilyushkin, Almalyk, Tashkent district.

M. Lezina, Doctor of Economics, answers:

The amount of meat consumed per head of population is measured by simply dividing the amount of meat bought by the total population. Meat sold through both State and co-operative outlets is counted, as well as meat bought at the agricultural produce markets, reared and used by small-holders and military units, and meat used in the food processing industry.

The amount of meat coming out of the abattoirs and of meat products includes pure meat, lard, category one and two side products, all agricultural animals and meat products (sausage, tinned meat products, rissoles, etc.).

The level of per capita consumption is different for every region of the country. It was above the All-Union [*i.e. USSR*] average for 1986 (62 kg.) in only six republics: the Russian Federation, 68 kg; the Ukraine, 67 kg; Byelorussia, 70 kg; the Baltic republics, over 80 kg. Typically these republics produced more meat per capita than they consumed. The Ukraine produced 21 per cent more, Byelorussia 51 per cent more, Lithuania 60 per cent more, Latvia 50 per cent more and Estonia 56 per cent more.

The remaining republics consume less meat per capita than the All-Union average. This level is especially low in the Central Asian republics (where they also produce far less). Uzbekistan consumes 29 kg. per capita; Tajikistan, 31 kg; Kirgizia, 42 kg.; Turkmenia, 43 kg. Then come the Transcaucasian republics: Azerbaijan, 36 kg.; Georgia, 47 kg; Armenia, 50 kg. Moldavia and Kazakhstan consume 58 and 61 kg. respectively.

The meat consumption levels in each republic mainly depend on how well developed their agricultural sectors are. During the first five years of the USSR Food Programme (1982–86), the gross output of all sectors rose by 11 per cent. In Byelorussia it rose by 18 per cent, in Lithuania and Latvia by 17 per cent, in Uzbekistan by 4 per cent, in Tajikistan by 5 per cent, in Turkmenia by 9 per cent, in Georgia and Armenia by 8 and 9 per cent respectively.

Of course one must be aware that the different republics specialize in different areas, thus contributing to the overall All-Union picture. For example, whereas the consumption of meat per head of population in Uzbekistan is 38 per cent more than they produce, the other side of the coin is that they produce 70 per cent more vegetables, melons and pumpkins than they consume. Even so, the meat consumption in each region depends to a great deal on how efficiently local reserves and resources are used in order to supplement the food supply.

CHAPTER FIVE

POLITICS AND MILITARY

In July 1990 Press censorship was finally abolished in the Soviet Union and freedom of the Press was enshrined in the constitution, on the US model. This was good news for – among millions of others – Mikoja Ripko, editor of Pravda of Transcaucasia, and the sports fans among his readership. His three-man censorship committee had a list of 200 firms who did work for the army and whose names were never to appear in the paper. 'It became absurd,' explained Ripko, 'when the results of football matches from these factories were published. As the name of only one of the teams appeared nobody knew who that team had beaten – or by whom it had been beaten.' More absurd still, presumably, when two such factory teams played each other.

Argumenty i Fakty, like many publications, has experienced the rather more sinister side. As recently as October 1988, with perestroika allegedly purging the ghosts of persecution, editor Starkov's head was on the block. President Gorbachev wanted his resignation for an opinion poll he had published on the popularity of Soviet People's Deputies. Andrei Sakharov came first, with Gorbachev in fifth place. The President likened the country to a sea of petrol and Argumenty i Fakty the match. Starkov refused to resign (unheard of) and the staff publicly threatened to strike in his support (unimaginable). 'Miners may strike,' said deputy editor Alexander Meshchersky, 'but journalists, never.'

Starkov survived and in the doing received more than fifty invitations from all over the Soviet Union to stand as a People's Deputy. He stood in Moscow and won on the first ballot. Meshchersky was another of the six successful reformist Argumenty i

*Fakty candidates. The furore had a useful side benefit for the
newspaper too – subscriptions increased from twenty-two to more
than thirty-three million.*

*The days of shadow writing – the messages between the lines –
have finally gone in the USSR. And so has the necessity of using
the readers as a shield, posing the awkward questions and using
readers' letters to justify the temerity. There are now no closed
areas of discussion (although a vigorous criticism of Lenin might
test that claim to its fullest) and the galvanic changes reverberating
through the country, and from it, provide an enormous agenda for*
Argumenty i Fakty's *readership. Perestroika, privilege, Gorbachev, the KGB, the army, the rehabilitation of Stalin's purged, the
remit of the party, Jewish emigration – the torrent of letters,
7,000 a day and rising, continues. 'The people have found their
tongue,' says Starkov. To which some in power might add 'the
bastards'.*

I am a victim. I live in a provincial city, Tcherkasa, that's
why I don't put my signature because, you understand, we
all know one another.

Don't let our young people go to capitalist countries. Why?
I had the chance to go to the United States on an exchange
basis. I used to be a true patriot of our country and I turned
into something really horrible. I became a human being. I
think; I have my own opinions; it's a nightmare.

After what I saw in the USA it's impossible to live here.
I'm not yet eighteen and I know that I won't do anything
good for our society. I had a desire to serve my country but I
don't have it any more. Because one person cannot change a
whole system.

I sympathize with Gorbachev, but deep in my heart I am
no longer a Soviet citizen and I don't care what's going on in
the USSR and I don't believe in anything in this country. The
question of whether we are worse off than they are doesn't
bother me any more. Yes, we are worse off because we live
like this.

I am a victim of what I saw and I know that I shall leave
this country. It's not mine any more.

So, don't allow the young people to go to capitalist
countries if you don't want to lose your future.

NOWADAYS, Russian towns and villages are witnessing a revival of the past glory and prestige of Russia (RSFSR). Therefore, we can ask the question: where should Russia's political centre be situated? According to the media, Moscow is going to be the capital city of Russia. We are categorically against it. There are two privileged cities in the Soviet Union: Moscow and Leningrad. The whole country works in order to keep them in the style to which they are accustomed. The whole country travels there to buy food and clothes. There, foreign artists give their performances and all big functions, contests, festivals and exhibitions take place. The rest of the country is merely a useful appendage to these two cities.

In our country, where fairness, justice and equality are supposed to rule, citizens are divided into categories according to where they happen to live. Hence the animosity between the provinces and the two cities. The discrimination against the provinces must be stopped. It is time for other Russian towns to regain their previous position and prestige.

If Moscow is made the capital city of the RSFSR, its local government will be under tremendous pressure from the central USSR government, and from the ministries which will officiate in Moscow.

Therefore we suggest that one of the ancient Russian towns whose old glory has been lost in present times be chosen as the capital city of the RSFSR. By doing so, we shall restore the greatness of at least one other Russian town and strengthen its political and cultural significance. There are many ancient cities to choose from: Vladimir, Yaroslavl, Suzdal, Ryazan and others.

We believe that a national referendum should be carried out in this matter.

> A. Golovin and others (eight signatures in all),
> Kamyshin, Volgagrad province.

MY name is Arkady. I am Jewish. I live in a smallish town in the Ukraine. There are few Jewish people in our locality, yet we feel threatened, like all other Jews in the Soviet Union. The government knows full well why we feel threatened and we no longer believe in their assurances. Many of us have known for a long time that there is no place for us here. I am no chauvinist, nor a nationalist fanatic, I am an ordinary man. But all my life I've had to suffer abuse and insults even from my neighbours. We were dirty Jews who would, sooner or later, be sent packing.

To cut it short, I do not intend to present my case to you in full, or try to convince you of anything.

The fact is that my wife and I have known for a long time that we want to emigrate to Israel. There is a problem, however. We have some savings, all hard-earned, honest money (not stolen from some poor Russian or Ukrainian). My father has worked as a carpenter all his life, I work in a factory, my sister is an accountant. I have no time to trudge from shop to shop in search of goods to buy, my mother can hardly walk at all these days, my father has severe asthma and skin cancer (Chernobyl legacy), everything is on my shoulders.

As an honest man, I want to ask why I am not allowed to sell out and exchange all my roubles for hard currency so I can take my savings with me when I leave. I have come to the conclusion that there is no other way but to look for a black-market currency dealer and let him change my money. I know that there is a hard currency shortage in the Soviet Union. On the other hand, I don't want to lose my life's savings. The State will not gain anything from my shady deal. On the contrary, it's a loss of prestige.

Many people see the State as a blood-sucking leech. It may be a strong comparison, but this is what young émigrés say about the Soviet Union abroad. I would like to take my savings with me, openly and honestly, without resorting to wheeler-dealers.

Kiev.

I am a professional soldier and have recently been relocated. I had to give up my flat, and they 'can't promise me anything' in the new place. My furniture and all my possessions are stored in a five-ton container vehicle, parked illegally in the yard. The penalty is R5 per day. Two months have passed and so far I've had to pay R300. This is a great deal of money to me. But there is nowhere I can put my things. Why can't the Ministry of Defence pay the fine? It is not my fault. Also, I can't afford to pay it, being the sole earner in my family.

Yuryev, Leningrad.

IT is a well-known fact that people in ex-socialist countries have had to suffer a considerable drop in living standards: a necessary measure accompanying the change to free market economy.

The governments of those countries have appealed to their citizens for patience and understanding in these difficult times, giving them an honest appraisal of the situation and how long they will have to suffer these hardships. In our country, the communist structure is being dismantled, but no new ideology has been provided for us. In some areas, attempts are being made to substitute State ideology with religious ideals, depending on local requirements.

A new way of life and a new economy cannot be constructed without substantial losses and a fair deal of trauma. It's a shame that our government did not take the trouble to explain this to us when it made the decision to exchange the socialist ideology of 'a glowing future' for the misty horizons of a market economy.

A. Prikhodko, Minsk.

SO much constructive critical written work is relegated to the bottom drawer or even to the wastepaper basket. A mass of talent and a great deal of practical solutions are hidden in forgotten students' theses and ignored improvement projects. We waste a lot of intellectual energy and resources investigating things already researched and documented in heedlessly rejected material. The Chinese, even before the Cultural Revolution, used to collect thousands of recipes and formulae of folk medicine and make use of them.

And what about us? Even now, no one would dare to collect such material, let alone publish it. Yet this is a foolish and wasteful attitude, pearls before swine. Our scientists, supposedly the representatives of the most advanced science in the world, would rather die than admit that there may be something of value in the mysterious practices of farmers, blacksmiths, carpenters, farriers and healers.

Who will be brave enough to compile an encyclopaedia of folklore, or a data bank of original ideas? The Znanie Society [*former publishers of* AIF] could help, for a start. Students and people interested in the subject could do the collecting of information. There is an inexhaustible wealth of knowledge. Just give people the address and you will be snowed under with truly fascinating material.

P. Rybalsky, Tolyatti.

THANKS to television, millions of people in all parts of the Soviet Union were able to discover the true nature of the majority of Leningrad active party members as shown at the party conference held in Tavrichesky Palace.

The first speaker was Boris Nikolaevich Nikolsky, the widely respected editor of *Neva* magazine and a People's Deputy. He spoke about the fate of the people who survived the Siege of Leningrad. The majority of them live in communal flats, often with no amenities. There is very little chance of their living standards improving in the future.

The majority of conference members received Nikolsky's address with no applause. On the contrary, they began slamming into him. Nikolsky appealed to his party comrades to listen. The matter was a national tragedy; it concerned old and unfortunate people who had gone through enough misery to last them a lifetime.

He was not allowed to continue. Shouts, boos, abuse, followed.

How can one expect compassion and concern about people's needs from party members who behave like that?

The first secretary of the party regional committee was more than a little embarrassed by his comrades' behaviour, and after the break, tried his hardest to mend matters.

During the USSR People's Deputies national elections, Leningrad communists suffered considerable losses. The latest disgraceful episode in Tavrichesky Palace gives us grounds to expect that at the forthcoming elections to the local councils, they'll do even worse.

Yu Popov, soldier on the Leningrad Front, member of CPSU
from 1951.

RECENTLY a Muscovite wrote to you asking if it was possible to buy a good government for hard currency. Well, I have another proposal which will bring us loads of hard currency. We should sell the Politburo and the Central Committee of the CPSU to the USA. Americans, being extremely practical, will then give us as much hard currency as we want. Why? Because they can then install these demagogues and obscurantists in the Japanese economy. The result of which would be that in two years there will be only reminiscences of the dominance of Japanese goods in the US market.

R. Nasiro, Naberezhnye Chelny, Tarat Republic.

NOWADAYS there is mass rehabilitation of victims of Stalin's repressions. Why do only KGB officials do this, referring back to their files for the information? A judge then makes a decision in each case on the material that they provide. It's a paradox. Because in the past, under the leadership of the party, these same KGB officials provided damning information and the same judges rubber-stamped it. What were their motives then? What are they now? And are they keeping to the law now or not . . . ?

Plotinha, Dushambe.

WHAT we have dreamed about for years in our country has not come true. Once again, power is concentrated in the hands of a president. And my point is not just about the president but about sixteen members of the presidential council too, ten of whom are members of the Central Committee of the CPSU and the Politburo. What a sham of democracy. How can we speak about pluralism of opinions if whatever you debate about, in the end the dictatorship of the CPSU prevails? Article Six of the constitution (the leading role of the CPSU) has been cancelled, but in fact it isn't so. Why has there been all this fuss about it? If the CPSU can just violate the constitution of the USSR what are the rest of us to do? We should act, divide and take power.

F. Kavalenka, war veteran, pensioner, State farm, Moscovski.

(*Since this letter was written the situation has changed. The*

166

elected heads of the republics form the majority on the presidential council. President Gorbachev, by contrast, remains elected to his position only by the party – Ed.)

SEVERAL times in *AIF* you have published data on subscriptions to different newspapers and magazines. The theory is that from this we can judge the popularity of different publications. But this isn't actually so. For example, in July our party committee let the different sections of our plant know about obligatory subscriptions to some of the newspapers and magazines. In particular, to *Pravda, Communist, Political Education* and some others. If the top level is stimulating the forced popularization of such publications – and our party committee is not the only one doing this sort of thing! – then the subscription data published by you loses its credibility. At the very least you should give some additional information alongside.

L. Belov, Radio Plant, Pensa.

I, and I suppose many other readers, have a question: why are the main celebrations in Moscow held at a cemetery. I mean the cemetery near the Kremlin's wall. Guest rostrums are near the graves of the outstanding figures of our country. Our leaders in a festive mood are on top of a sarcophagus with Lenin's body inside. There is nothing like this in any other country. And none of us would allow such treatment of our own relatives.

To my mind this senseless decision made by Stalin and his cohorts needs revising. The prestige of our leaders wouldn't be lost if government and guest rostrums during celebrations were installed on the opposite side of Red Square.

V. Artemchuk, senior scientific worker, Zheleznodorozhnyy.

I want to resign as a human being. I joined the military college voluntarily but I can't resign voluntarily. When I became a student at the college I did not sign any documents, or papers on the terms of service. Nowhere did it say that I had to give to the army twenty-five years. It is said that in cases of illness people can resign, but I'm healthy. Or they can be dismissed for discrediting the rank of officer but I am honestly fulfilling my duties. Is it the same for officers as field engineers that they can make a mistake only once? [*A Soviet saying has it that sappers never make a mistake or they make it only once – and they're dead – Ed.*]

E. Gasparov, Kharkov.

TO deal with national disturbances in our republics (Armenia, Georgia, Nagorny Karabakh) the regular army is used. The army's role has always been the protection of the State against outside enemies. None of the civilized states has ever used the regular army to suppress inner disorders. We know that the Tsarist governments' use of army forces against workers and demonstrators caused a lot of dissatisfaction among army officers at that time, and among the high State officials, including deputies of the Duma [*contemporary parliament – Ed.*].

In other countries, apart from the police there are special divisions – like in the USA with the National Guard – who are deployed against internal disorder. For the same purpose we too have our so-called inner forces. I am quite sure that the use of the regular army for the suppression of different kinds of disorders inside the country is very harmful and dangerous and the consequences can be very unpredictable. It discredits the army in front of the people. It helps to develop a feeling among people that the army is a threat. It is a humiliation to the army, this role is not in its tradition.

If there is a shortage in inner forces, special divisions should be developed as soon as possible for this and they should be directly responsible to the President and the Supreme Soviet, but the army should not struggle against the people.

V. Turbakov, Vladivostok.

WHY is it that delegations of the Supreme Soviet of the USSR travelling abroad are headed by members of the Politburo. For instance, in Japan Comrade Yakovlev, in Britain

Comrade Medvedev and so on. They are only People's Deputies and not even members of the Supreme Soviet. I think these delegations should be headed by chairmen of chambers or their deputies, by chairmen of commissions, committees, or their deputies. But in these cases we witness again that the party is fighting to carry out roles which do not belong to it and continues even to lead the People's Deputies of the USSR.

N. Brelev, Statriascol, Belgorodskaya region.

THE Central Committee of the CPSU has proclaimed that it's impossible to have any unlawful privileges for party members. There are certain doubts, however, concerning the preservation of the privilege system for medical services for apparatchiks and the Central Committee and the Council of Ministers of the USSR. We are communists of the all-union Scientific Research Institute and condemn the preservation of such a system and that is why we address to the Central Committee of the CPSU this demand to give district party organizations lists of all convalescent homes, rest homes, clinics and hospitals together with indications of their revenues and expenditures and the number of beds they have and the cost of rooms in them. We also demand that information about the distribution of vouchers for the above-mentioned establishments is given for different categories of party workers and for the workers and relatives of elected bodies.

This appeal was adopted at the meeting of the Leningrad party committee on 26 March 1990. Protocol 32.

THE communists of our workshop and all of the people of our enterprise are very angry because for a long time we have heard about social justice but there is no such thing and never has been. And we think that in our country there should be no convalescent homes for the Central Committee of the CPSU, or the Central Committee of the young communists or the all-union trade unions, or the Council of Ministers of the USSR, or the Supreme Soviet, or the Moscow executive committee – and so on. All the convalescent homes should be given to the trade unions and everybody should use their services, beginning with a worker in a collective farm up to the President of the USSR.

From the protocols of the meeting of the party organization,
workshop number 4, Formetal, Labinsk, Krasnodar.

IT doesn't matter how many bad things are said about Comrades Stalin, Yagadev, Khrushchev and Beria, I'll never believe them. Yes, Comrade Stalin was very severe and his power was very severe and when he was in power he shot a lot of people. He was quite right to do this. Who was shot? People's enemies. Let us thank him for all that. None of the common people, even those who were in camps, will say anything bad about him or suspect him of injustice.

Khalanga, Ilichovsk, Odessa.

I remember a party meeting of the Admiraltski plant in Leningrad at which I was present. The communist Ivanov put the question, why haven't party congresses been convened for many years, Lenin used to convene them each year? The next day comrade Ivanov did not appear at work. He disappeared.

A. Gusev, party veteran, Kiev.

IS the situation in our party so bad that it has to keep its members by force? If persuasion does not work, they are punished severely. What about democracy and freedom of choice?

My husband, I. F. Shelapailo, captain, military pilot first class, was taken off flight duty and transferred to another division for leaving the party. I want to ask you a question: all those years it was not the party but the people who paid my husband his salary and it was to the people that he vowed his allegiance. So what's the connection between party membership and a job flying?

Members of the military council were suspicious of his good record. 'Belenko also had a good record but suddenly flew over the border,' they said. They did not take into account that my husband could have done that more than once while serving in Afghanistan. When he lost faith in the party he openly left it rather than hide his feelings like many people do. Isn't that proof of his honesty? I think he was punished for other people's edification.

He stated his reason for leaving the CPSU in his resignation:

1. Inability to do something to correct major drawbacks in the country, army and party.

2. Reluctance to be with those who have been discrediting the party.

3. The incompetence and heel-dragging of most communists.

T. Shelapailo, Alma-Ata.

YOU have repeatedly raised the question of country cottages [*dachas*] for government officials. I would like to draw your attention to the following circumstance: it is often the case that former tenants of these dachas are given plots of land to build cottages with their own money. The procedure appears to be quite legal, even though it has been agreed that officials in certain posts should not have private dachas.

I am against the practice of granting plots of land for dachas at the government's request to persons who do not deserve such a privilege, some of whom have even disgraced themselves when they held State or government office.

For instance, at the request of former vice-chairman of the USSR Council of Ministers Murakhovsky, a plot of land on the territory of the State forestry reserve bordering the Novo-Daryino suburban settlement of the USSR Academy of Sciences (Odintsovo District) has been sold to Tsedenbal, former general secretary of the Mongolian People's Revolutionary Party Central Committee and chairman of the Praesidium of the People's Great Hural [*local parliament*]. Previously a dacha costing R600,000 was built for Tsedenbal in Zhukovka. Since his family was unable to pay, the Mongolian Embassy agreed to foot the bill. A question arises – for what services should a new plot of land be allotted to the person whom his own country demands to be called to account?

Next to Zhukovka, a plot of land has been given to V. Ulyanov, an APN [*news agency*] staff member, whose only 'merit' is that he is a grand-nephew of Vladimir Lenin.

How many generations have to pass before family ties cease to hypnotize us? What have all these people got to do with the USSR Academy of Sciences where more than seventy members are waiting for a plot of land in accordance with the government's resolution? Dachas for the above-mentioned people would automatically become part of the Academy's suburban settlement. In order to build them part of the forest had to be felled even though this has caused strong protests from the residents of nearby villages, the local rural Soviet and the inhabitants of the settlement. How much longer are we going to allow these 'exceptions to the rule'?

Academician V. Smirnov, chairman of the board of
administration, Novo-Daryino suburban settlement of the
USSR Academy of Sciences.

DESPITE glasnost and perestroika the KGB remains off limits and retains its old functions, goals, organization and, most importantly, opportunities. Before perestroika, this country's leaders could not do without such a body to keep them in power. Today our country is living through revolutionary changes which are opposed openly and covertly by the old guard. They stand in the way of many initiatives which lead to economic and political instability. It is officially recognized that perestroika has not yet become irreversible. What if future leaders return to Stalin's or Brezhnev's socialism?

Of all the known methods of cracking down on perestroika and its supporters, the KGB's unique opportunities are the most dangerous, effective and fast-acting. Why should the KGB have preserved these opportunities and its structure despite all the democratization?

V. Klokov, Moscow.

MORE than 100 persons resigned at a plenum of the CPSU Central Committee last spring (1988) but, with rare exceptions, none of them accepted blame or apologized for their behaviour.

'Do you want them to be put on trial or sent into exile?' some may ask me. No, I just want to call a spade a spade. For

172

example, when a regional party committee secretary resigns because he has failed to cope with his duties, messed up his work and discredited himself, this could be reported. We should not simply be told that he has been 'transferred to other duties'. Moral condemnation is needed not so much for the sacked party officials, since it's water off a duck's back, but for anyone who might want to follow their example and squander billions of roubles to the detriment of the nation.

A. Chaiko, Kiev.

I am a party member with a good record and everyone says that I was a conscientious worker who did social work enthusiastically. But I became older and my fire disappeared. I am not a fighter by nature and I have seen much injustice in life. On learning the truth about our past I was devastated.

My life is now confined to my family: the rest I do from habit – paying my dues, making reports. At meetings I always vote 'for' and keep silent most of the time. Does the party really need such a member? I am no longer 'an active fighter' but I cannot leave the party. It takes courage to hand in your party card. I am afraid. Not so much for myself as for my children. How will it affect their lives? Should I ask to be expelled from the party? But that is against the rules. Please tell me why you can join the party at your own request but cannot leave it that way? I do not think I am the only one. If the party got rid of us it would be smaller but purer.

I take it all very much to heart: if I remain in the party I will be dishonest, if I leave I will be disgraced. Because I am a disciplined person I cannot miss party meetings or ignore my duties and I religiously pay my dues so I am still considered a model communist.

N. R. Zarafshan.

THERE is much talk about the enemies of perestroika. Where are they? And who are they? I want to know their first names and surnames!

G.K., Buzuluk.

I have made up my mind to give up my privileged title ('the worker is owner of his country').

P. Permye.

EACH day, I and millions of viewers watching the title of *Time* [*news programme*] see a globe appear on the screen, then from our territory a star comes which symbolizes a satellite, then from the satellite a rocket is launched which makes a semicircle and lands on the territory of the USA. I assume it is just a coincidence. But what will the rest of the world think of all this?

D.Z., Dimitrov, Moscow region.

AT the head of the group sent to Kusbask to solve the problem of the miners' strike was a member of the Politburo, secretary of the Central Committee of the CPSU, N. Slinkov. Question. What is the legal authorization of Slinkov as he is not a member of the Supreme Soviet of the USSR or the Russian Federation or indeed a member of the government? I put my question not to Comrade Slinkov but to the people. Because it turns out to be a paradox. Some decisions are taken, they are carried out by other people and the responsible people are among a third group or in many cases 'nobody is responsible'.

Isn't one of the main reasons for the position we find ourselves in now that in very many vitally important problems the decisions are taken by people who do not have any legal or juridical responsibility to the people for the outcome? I am not trying to encroach upon the powers of the party, given that I have been a party member myself for twenty-six years, but I think that everyone should be held accountable for their decisions, otherwise it turns out that while the country teeters on the edge of disaster no one is responsible. I think that future generations will know the answers.

R. Koklin, Omsk.

I can't agree with the statement from the chairman of the Central Committee of the CPSU that the party does not get any State subsidies. Nowadays such subsidies are covered over as different enterprises and organizations have to provide party committees with free premises, equipment, facilities, heating and cleaning, radio communications and transport, all of this free of charge. Apart from that, the services of the typing pools and copying and mail services, all these are free of charge. And they purchase different office goods, different political and economic literature, they subscribe to periodicals and buy film and slides on the expenses of the enterprise. All of their propaganda activities are on the accounts of the collectives where they are. The enterprises give radio time free of charge to the party, if they have radio, and they are not charged for the publication of their newspapers.

So the collectives suffer losses due to the different kinds of meetings and conferences which the party members are involved in during normal working hours.

The party worker can't do all his work in his own time. In accordance with a modest estimate our plant with 360 communists annually spends on the above-mentioned things the sum of R10,000. In other words, twenty-eight roubles per communist. If our party organization is an average one – and that seems likely – then taking into account that we have eighteen million communists in our country then it means that State subsidies to the party exceed R500 million a year.

Unfortunately, subsidies at the same level are also given to the young communist league organizations, to the trade union organizations and other public organizations.

So what will happen to collectives with a multi-party system and with the growth of political and social organizations and societies? Those are the facts not guesses. It's necessary to adopt a law about parties, about social and political and voluntary organizations and to define their status and to ensure that they are maintained only by their dues and from voluntary contributions from the population. The collective membership should be abolished and this should be done before the adoption of the CPSU's code and that of other organizations.

V. Monyesev, head of department, superphosphate plant,
Jambur.

STALINISM is now criticized by everybody but up until now none of the official authorities – not at the twenty-second party congress, nor the nineteenth all-union party conference, nor the plenums of the Central Committee, nor the congress of People's Deputies of the USSR – has officially dissociated from Stalin or Stalinism and from the criminal party era. We have to condemn officially Stalin and Stalinism.

If it is possible fifty years later to legally rehabilitate those in the party who were illegally expelled then why isn't it possible to expel from the party and to publicly convict Stalin, Voroshilov, Molotov and all the party functionaries down to the district party level who by their criminal activities for the whole period of Stalinism compromised themselves and inflicted considerable moral and ideological harm on the party? Why do we communists have to be in the same party as Stalin and other political criminals?

And another very important point: up to what time will the criminals and killers, those who are to blame, who by their actions allowed Stalin to consolidate his power, lie next to Lenin's tomb? Those who created this ugly conception which the whole civilized world rightly calls Stalinism. I think that the liquidation of the memorial cemetery next to Lenin's tomb is not a secondary point and it has to be done in the near future and not put at the bottom of the pile.

B. Nikolaev, Kiev.

ALL Soviet constitutions have contained a great many declarations which actually mean nothing. My daughter married a cadet from the Leningrad military school and went to Leningrad. Yet she could neither get a job nor receive permanent resident status. She lost this status in her home city of Kerch. If you can't get it in Leningrad then no one will employ you.

Is this what you call the right to work? My daughter is going on maternity leave in a few months' time. As she has no job she will get nothing apart from a miserly twenty or thirty roubles a month. How is she supposed to live? She's most likely to come back to her parents in Kerch. This is a case study of Soviet human rights. Indeed hundreds of such women have no right to permanent resident status. How can they live, bear children and raise them for two years till their husbands graduate? No one will give them food stamps to receive rationed goods – soap, sugar, tea, meat, etc. – if they are not registered as permanent residents. For the same reason, health care will not be available. Who is responsible for the infringement of the constitutional right to work?

E. Meisner, Kerch.

(*The wonderful Soviet war photographer Dmitri Baltermants captured one of the most devastating and disturbing images of the Second World War in 1942 at Kerch. In a bleak, muddy, puddled landscape peasant women search across strewn bodies for relatives shot by Nazi murder squads – in the right of the picture a shawled old woman discovers a son or husband on the ground, on his back, his hands frozen in a final surrender. It is heartbreakingly affecting and seems, somehow, to sum up the cost the country paid opposing fascism.*

After the war, Stalin summoned the entire corps of Soviet war photographers and ordered them to destroy all of their negatives apart from those that he considered best represented the heroic struggle. Having endured almost unimaginable conditions, they were left with only three or four approved images. Baltermants, with incredible courage, was the only one to refuse. He died in 1990 – Ed.)

RECENTLY we carried out a survey at the Lenin Military-Political Academy on young officers' attitudes. The results of the survey show that a proportion of young, well-trained officers have expressed a desire to leave military service.

For example, in 1989 about 27 per cent of those who submitted requests for dismissal were under twenty-three; approximately 43 per cent, twenty-three to twenty-five; 21 per cent, twenty-five to thirty and the rest over thirty. An analysis of the data obtained shows that about 77 per cent of the officers who want to leave the military are efficient and show initiative. Of those submitting resignations 90 per cent had been classed as good or excellent students at the military schools (one quarter were rated 'excellent'); over 16 per cent of the officers had served in the army as soldiers and sergeants before they entered the higher educational establishments;

65 per cent are communists and approximately 21 per cent young communists.

The analysis shows that about 10 per cent of those who tendered their resignation had no confidence in their futures.

The main causes of dissatisfaction are living standards as well as social and cultural grievances. At present skilled workers receive much higher pay than army officers. Taking into account communal troubles in military garrisons and the problem of job placement for officers' wives, many families find they have to live on the husbands' pay alone and cannot make ends meet.

Expenditure on housing is the biggest burden for most servicemen's families. Every fourth officer applying to leave military service lived with his family in a rented privately owned dwelling. The families of every third platoon commander and deputy commander of a company for political affairs, who have decided to leave the army, live in the same conditions. More than 60 per cent are dissatisfied with their earnings.

While the pay factor is the most important for young officers, the reasons for resignation given by officers with more than five years' service are usually linked with the impossibility of finding jobs for their wives and places at preschool centres for their children, as well as the shortage of essential goods.

The widespread view that it is mainly young single officers who are leaving the service is not borne out by the figures for this group of 12.5%.

Much is being done within the army and navy to resolve the questions raised in this short review: pay is being increased and additional sums are earmarked for paying rent, etc. However, society as a whole must work to restore the loss of prestige suffered by those serving in the armed forces if the trend of resignations is to be reversed.

S. Syedin, head of department; V. Mukhin, student, Lenin Military-Political Academy.

THE CPSU Central Committee journal *Politicheskoye Obrazovaniye* carried an article entitled 'Defending the Interests of the Socialist Motherland'. The article said, in part, 'The fundamental organizational principles for the development of the Soviet Armed Forces include unity of command, regarded by Lenin as the most advisable method of leadership in the armed forces.'

However, the party was in no position to translate it into practice at once. At the time of the Civil War and foreign military intervention the party invited a considerable number of military specialists trained before the Revolution to serve in the Red Army. By the mid-1920s more than 48,000 former generals and officers of other ranks had been called up. The commanders-in-chief of the armed forces of the fledgling Soviet republic during the Civil War were former Tsarist colonels I. L. Vatsetic and S. S. Kamenev. Twenty people from among military specialists were appointed commanders of groups of armies and more than eighty army commanders. Specialists needed to be under party control, with the Institution of Commissars created for the purpose. Without the commissar's signature no order issued by the commander could be carried out.

Over the past seventy-two years the Institution of Commissars has developed into the Chief Political Department of the Army and Navy complete with its own personnel department and unaccountable to the USSR Ministry of Defence. Thirteen political academies have come into being. This entire machine is intended to control the army and navy – the original function of the Institution of Commissars set up in 1918.

Degrading treatment of recruits in the army and navy is a great talking point today. But why shouldn't we mention those who brought about a situation in which junior commanding officers, all the way up to company commander, have been robbed of disciplinary powers? And again, as the armed forces are reduced, it is those not to the liking of the political bodies who are being made redundant. When will the unity of command principle which Lenin considered the most appropriate for the armed forces be implemented?

A. Ananishin, Riga.

I have always thought that the participation in demonstrations was a purely voluntary thing but not long ago this conviction was shattered. The administration of the Rostov factory punished its workers for not taking part in the demonstrations on 1 May and 7 November. Those who didn't attend lost a tenth of the thirteenth salary [*a traditional annual month's bonus*] and those that missed both lost 20 per cent.

Petrova, Rostov.

FOR three and a half years I have been working as an instructor at the October District Committee of the Communist party of Moscow and I happen to be a witness and a participant in the acute political struggle in our society. When I got acquainted with the Democratic Platform in the CPSU published in *Pravda* on 3 March 1989, I realized that this particular platform has common sense and gives a possibility to get out of the deadlock. That's why I became a convinced supporter of its main principles, though this platform has some shortcomings.

I declared my convictions openly on 4 April at a party meeting. None of those present criticized me but they said that it was our duty to support and propagandize the platform of the Central Committee. Of course, that's what we're paid for! When I attended party organizations I expressed my standpoint and on most occasions I got support and approval from the communists. What's more, the communists of three party organizations put forward my candidacy to the twenty-eighth Congress and the Moscow City party conference. My competitor was Muravlov, secretary of the Central Committee of the CPSU.

But on 11 April an open letter to the communists of the country was published. On the same day I was called to the office of the secretary of the district committee by Muravlov, and in the presence of Rosin, who is in charge of the organization department, he told me that he was speaking to me on the instructions of the first and second secretaries of the district committee of the CPSU. At the beginning of the talk he asked me if I had read the published letter. Then he asked me if I continued to support the Democratic Platform. I answered in the affirmative. Then I was told to find another job. No serious grounds for discharging me were given. Such is the level of democracy in one of the central districts of Moscow.

L. Hanev, Moscow.

LAST year a special commission consisting of People's Deputies of the USSR investigated the Bilesi tragedy. Yegor Ligachev was accused, while Mikhail Gorbachev was away, that he held a sitting with a small group of members of the Politburo of the Central Committee of the CPSU and behind the back of Mikhail Gorbachev took a decision to use army units in the Bilesi events. None of the members of the Politburo – including Gorbachev, Ryzhkov, Sheverdnadze – corrected the mistake and allowed false rumours to be spread and it was only at the plenum in February 1990 that it was revealed that all the members of the Politburo took part in the sitting and that Mikhail Gorbachev, Ryzhkov and Sheverdnadze attended the sitting too.

So it becomes clear that it was decided that Ligachev become a scapegoat. The main thing is that it was decided to mislead public opinion.

Cheshin, Lomolasev, Leningrad region.

THE interview given by President Gorbachev in connection with the election of Boris Yeltsin as chairman of the Supreme Soviet of the Russian Federation surprised me greatly. The statement by the President to the effect that they might have chosen a better candidate is, to put it mildly, not ethical towards the chairman of the Russian Federation and it is insulting to those who voted for him, to say nothing of the 85 per cent of the population of the Russian Federation who are supporting him.

The President seems to have forgotten by what quorum he was elected himself [*he was elected by the party and has been widely criticized for not standing for open election*] to his present post.

I believe the President should be more polite to the leaders of the republics which are gaining their sovereignty and he should not suspect them of any political intrigues. In the near future the confederation of sovereign republics will determine not only the policy but the composition of the central power.

The statements by the President set me thinking. Well, Mikhail Sergeevich, you have been in charge for five years and what can we see around us? The time of illusions has passed but I personally haven't lost hope. I talked to many of my friends about this and none of them approved of what the President said. Many of them said, Mikhail, you are not right.

Babiak, professor.

WHAT was it on 16 and 18 January 1990 in the North Caucasian military district when about 20,000 military reservists were alerted and flown to Armenia? On 19 January the commander of the North Caucasian military district on the instruction of the war minister Yazov declared on the radio that the call-up was cancelled and those who were called up should return to their enlistment offices in five days' time. One would like to ask Comrade Yazov and other generals what it was. Was it just training? It couldn't be just training because the notice was too short and too many men were involved. Was it a mobilization? Well, under the constitution of the USSR it can be announced only by the Supreme Soviet of the USSR. A mobilization is, in effect, a recognition of an unannounced civil war.

The military cannot give any convincing reasons for the call-up and its cancellation three days later. In fact, the call-up was cancelled because of the unrest and protest meetings against it among the Russian population of the Stavropol-Krasnodarsk and Rostov regions and the outbreaks of hostility towards Armenians and Azerbaijanis who live in those regions. There was a real danger of turning the North Caucasus into a new hotbed of national conflicts. Now with the participation of the Russian population it means that the flame of civil war might have spread all over the country crossing the Caucasian mountains.

It was only ten years after that we learned who involved the Soviet Union in the war in Afghanistan and now we want to know who wanted to repeat Afghanistan within the borders of the USSR. And we also want to know who managed to stop our ardent generals. In the hardest time for our country, 20,000 young people were alerted and flown to another republic. It would be only fair if Comrade Yazov and his generals paid the expenses from their own pockets. And how about the moral damage?

Soblev, Nova Alexandrovsk.

ALL social organizations – the Komsomol [*young communists*], various sporting societies, the Red Cross, to say nothing of the party – collect their dues themselves. But such mass organizations like trade unions with numerous staff have become so bureaucratic, incompetent and inactive that they appealed to the government to impose the task of collecting dues on the management of enterprises, organizations and institutions. It's ridiculous, no trade union in the world has such a practice. It contradicts the very idea of trade unions. In fact the trade union leaders dance Pavlovian before the management of enterprises, said Mikhail Gorbachev. And how can they behave differently if the management, through the accounting department, collects 1 per cent of the salaries and wages from all their workers and employees, no matter whether they are members of the trade union or not?

As for the trade unions, they dispose of the money the way they like. The leaders get high salaries, prizes, holiday accommodation vouchers and they have other benefits. The workers and employees can get a holiday voucher only once in fifty years. The question is, why should the workers and employees be divided into members of trade unions and non-members if they have to pay dues just the same? Can't the new leaders of the trade unions understand that they should be economically and politically independent and that they must defend the rights and interests of the workers and employees, not in words but in reality?

Sharipov, Alma Ata.

OVER the last few years we have been talking a lot about the strengthening of discipline. People's Deputies often dwell on the subject too. But unfortunately their words are at variance with their deeds. One can't help but be surprised when one watches the sessions. Some people walk, some people read, some people talk to their neighbours and some are just having a nap. And these are our deputies whose task is to solve the most important problems of our country.

As for their participation in the work of the session, the situation is like this: for example, at the second congress 2,106 deputies were registered. On some days only 1,780 deputies took part in the work. Where were the rest? Didn't they think that their presence was necessary?

One day a hockey match was being held and a People's Deputy, a well-known singer called Copson, was shown. He was rooting for the national team of the USSR. At the same time a session of the congress was being held. During the voting one could see a deputy voting for two persons. It means that there were fewer deputies than registered. They talk a lot about discipline but they violate it themselves and millions of people see it.

Garayev, Yaroslavl.

*(It works two ways. Live televising of paraliament had to be ended because too many people were taking time off work to watch —
Ed.)*

NEWSPAPERS, magazines, the radio and TV programmes often criticize the cult of personality of Stalin, the stagnation period of the Brezhnev time; they criticize careerists, fawners, bribe-takers but all this is in the past tense. One might think they didn't exist any more.

We brand Stalin with shame for his repressions and butchery. I am also a victim of the Stalin regime in a way. But Stalin is not the only person who is to blame for all this. The people who surrounded him are to blame too. There were fawners and climbers when Khrushchev was in power. And where were the leaders surrounding Brezhnev when he promoted himself, hung gold stars upon himself and even awarded himself the Order of Victory? Why didn't anybody tell him it was absurd?

The newspaper *Izvestia* of 11 January 1989 carries an article entitled 'We Had Better Not Return to the Past'. 'It was unpleasant to hear,' the author points out, 'what the First Secretary of the Ural Regional Committee said: "Everything was done in accordance with your instructions Mikhail Sergeevich." And it was unpleasant when some of the participants just read out prepared texts.' There is another example.

A women's Arctic team, Mitelitsa, sent New Year wishes to Mikhail Gorbachev. 'Dear Mikhail Sergeevich, we wish you and Raisa Maximovna a Happy New Year, we wish you good health,' and so on. I wonder why they forgot to mention the rest of the family. Well, isn't this fawning?

Once they were showing on TV the visit of Nikolai Ryzhkov to one of the plants of Kemerova. Special preparations had been made for the occasion. Everything was freshly painted. Seeing this Nikolai Ivanovich said, 'I don't like this window dressing.' And he said the right thing. I am all for perestroika, but without fawners, climbers or bribe-takers who only interfere with progress.

Tikhanov, Minsk.

THE law passed in the USSR on the honour and dignity of the President [*it is a criminal offence to insult the office*] could be looked upon in different ways. It might be a prelude to the appearance of a new genius, the wisest of the wise. The assertion that criticizing the President's activities and the policies pursued under his leadership will be quite legal under the new law is nothing but utopia because practice shows that the most objective criticism is usually considered to be an insult which will have unpredictable consequences on the one who criticizes. It appears that the honour and dignity of the President is based not on his real authority but on fines, deportations and other oppressive measures.

In fact, the honour and dignity of the President depends on the standard of living of the people. The President himself should think of his authority but not repressive organs. Besides they shouldn't have revealed that the monthly pay of the President is R4,000 while people who fought at the Front in the Great Patriotic War and worked hard all their lives now live in poverty. It looks like the main problem of our time is not getting out of our deadlock but protecting the honour and dignity of 'his excellency'.

Dutko, pensioner, City of Chirkasa.

I read an article which was an interview with Yegor Ligachev. The title of the article puzzled me: 'Socialism Has Enormous Resources and It Cannot be Improved by Capitalism'. How come it cannot be improved by capitalism? That is just what we are doing. We are using modern Western technology building joint enterprises and co-operatives – even potatoes are grown on the basis of Dutch know-how and there is nothing bad about it. Different political systems should enrich and supplement each other. We shall only win. And one more just society will be created. Maybe it's utopia but one wants to believe that it could be so.

It doesn't matter what name that society bears, it's important that all of the people should live under good conditions and that there is justice for everyone. To achieve all this we must work hard but this doesn't suit many high-ranking officials. Why should they work if they already live in a communist society? For them perestroika is an end to their paradise. That's why they sabotage and put all kinds of obstacles in the way of progress.

In the country there is an acute shortage of food products, medicine and equipment. We buy all this abroad and the imported goods rot at the ports and railway stations. Where is our leadership, which has been entrusted with power? Why don't they punish those who are responsible for this state of affairs? Our people already understand what is what. When the leaders speak from their rostrums they are for perestroika but in their studies they make a mess of the whole thing and they stimulate the crime rate. They hope to lead the people to despair so that they would strangle it with their own hands but they are mistaken – people believe in perestroika and there is no way back.

Kolesnikov, Novosibirsk.

WE, people of the village of Shatinskaya, are against citizens of the Korean People's Democratic Republic working in the territory of our village and the Vertnibrayn district as a whole. We can understand that our government is interested in getting more timber but we see here how high the price is. They fell trees injuriously to the wooded areas. And they cause great damage to our fauna. They catch sables and they steal sables from our hunters. They dam rivers and catch fish using poaching methods. They also sell home-made vodka and other things.

It's painful seeing our land being devastated. We want to leave something for our children and grandchildren so we are against citizens of the Korean People's Democratic Republic working in this territory.

Logniva, on behalf of the people of the village of Shatinskaya, the Hubarov region.

MY nephew went to serve in the army. He began to study at the school of sergeants in the town of Chernovsi. On the first day of his arrival the older boys stole everything from him so that he only had slippers left. They took everything, including his razor and a cake of soap. Nobody wanted to investigate the case. Alexander wrote a letter to his parents and his father brought him everything he asked him to bring including a brush and a razor. But a few days later he was beaten again and robbed. They took everything his father brought him. I have been subscribing to your newspaper for several years and I see that it gives much coverage to the problem. But the state of affairs doesn't change.

I have a son who will serve in the army in three years and we want to save him from this. How long shall we send our sons to the army for such humiliation? How long will you get such letters?

Bucherov, City of Narilsk.

I have a newspaper, *Flag of our Motherland*, of the Black Sea fleet dated 24 February 1953. The name of Stalin is mentioned forty-two times on the front page. One can remember that in the time of Khrushchev or Brezhnev the portraits and articles of those leaders appeared practically every day in newspapers and magazines and it was considered almost to be a crime if speaking at a meeting one didn't quote what was said. Well, now I take as an example the newspaper *Izvestia* of last May. The portraits of Gorbachev appear in practically every issue (1, 2, 8, 9, 13, 15, 16, 17, 19, 22, 26 and 30).

In the paper of 30 May his portrait appears even in advertisements – the front page was not enough!

Does history repeat itself?

Fyodorov, Gorky.

WHAT country of the world has more than one president? Why does the Soviet Union need another fifteen besides the President of the USSR? What duties will they have and what will be the duties of the main president? Will it be another collective leadership or will the USSR be divided into separate states?

Well, we have chairmen of the Supreme Soviets of the Republics, why do we need presidents? It puzzles and it arouses indignation. When will the government start thinking of the common people? A presidential committee has been set up, it is composed of the same people, the élite of the period of stagnation. We need good specialists and clever and efficient economists. If we haven't got any in this country perhaps it would be better to invite some from civilized and prospering countries so they could help us out of the deadlock.

The manipulations in the leadership don't mislead anyone. Everyone understands what is going on. All this can lead to nothing good, but a civil war. We are not sure of tomorrow and we are afraid for our children and grandchildren. There is a lot of talk in the leadership but no steps are made to overcome the crisis. Everything is directed at the seizure of power and the preservation of power and privileges. Who will solve this problem? Who will remember the common people?

Dedanova, labour veteran, member of the CPSU, City of
Chelyabinsk.

PEOPLE are arguing nowadays about what kind of party we should have, or how many parties we should have – one or many? I want to ask, do we really need a party at all, any party, communist, democratic, republican, labour? What for? I can see that a teacher teaches, a doctor treats patients, a peasant ploughs, a builder builds. What about the party? It collects party dues, it arranges plenums, it works out new political tendencies – can it be called work, and who can give a guarantee that the new political tendency will prove to be correct? How does the party know that the people must follow this political line and no other? If we look at the history of the Communist party we can see that its policies always led into blind alleys. Isn't it more realistic to live in accordance with economic and social laws? Maybe the Politburo and its secretaries should go to work in the mines, in the fields, on construction sites, in the plants, and produce material products with their hands and not with their tongues.

I believe we badly need a democratic State with clever and just laws in all spheres of life and mechanisms which make these laws effective. The party is just a ship which is sailing where its captain guides it. First it was the Lenin party, then it was the Stalin party, then it was the Brezhnev party and now, if Gorbachev repairs it a little, it will be the Gorbachev party.

It was very kind of Gorbachev to allow us to talk on various themes but supposing another communist comes to power, a cruel and immoral man. The party will bear his name and will salute him and it will lead the people again into physical and spiritual slavery. We haven't got rid of it yet. Perhaps we should separate any party from the State so that one's membership of the party could not influence one's career or material wellbeing, as it has done with the Church? There was a time when people were not promoted if they were religious and if they were communists they were promoted and got lots of other benefits from the State.

Traskina, a worker.

NOW it seems that we can shout out loud that the diagnosis of that long and exhausting disease – as a result of which Russia found itself on the brink of catastrophe – turned out to be Bolshevism. The recovery will be slow and hard. The attention of the peoples of Russia is concentrated on the work of our parliament and the fate of our country depends on it. However, these sessions of all the parliaments invariably take place under the shadow of a huge stone idol [*Marx*].

Is it in accordance with freedom of conscience, freedom of religious belief? Nowadays, anyone can pray to any god he likes. Well, who will bear the responsibility of the great tragedy suffered by Russia? That ghost who has been haunting Europe and other countries on the planet for 150 years? Or maybe some real people?

Rianov, Petrograd.

BORIS Yeltsin in his article 'I'm Still An Optimist' speaks about the private planes for the nightingales of perestroika, that is, for the party élite. Let's count how much this pleasure costs for our State budget. The maintenance of a plane – Ilyushin 62 or 2134 – is about R100–120,000 a month. The total number of members and alternate members of the Politburo and secretaries of the Central Committee of the CPSU is about 100. It means that the maintenance of private planes is about R10–12 million a month and not less than R100–150 million a year. Our political leaders like to say that they are trying to find means to help our common Soviet beggars to return to our democratic paradise!

Grishin, Sebastopol.

GORBACHEV needs nationwide help with perestroika. What is he getting instead? Sabotage, rampant mismanagement, irresponsibility and slackness everywhere. Information on it comes every day. The whole nation is indignant at the moral and material damage done to every one of us. We hear voices from the top promising punishment to the culprits – but we all know it's sheer talk. Not that we want Stalin's atrocities but it's high time to drop our permissiveness. Strict discipline is what we need.

What I propose is a year or two of convict camps (as minimum punishment) for sabotage, mismanagement and slapdash work. All bosses – even the biggest – must be liable. If they don't work honestly for perestroika, we'll make them!

It will be a temporary measure to bring things into order. Enough talk, it's time to strike one's fist. This is the only possible way to do things now. 'But then, we have our law,' you may say. The law? Who cares about it? It takes emergency legislation to frighten the bosses and everybody else into proper work.

R. Chervonova, Ryazan.

AT our plant, party meetings are held during working hours and since its different production units stand miles apart, office transport is used for carrying CPSU members to the meeting. The situation with trade union meetings is the same. This means that we are wasting away the pay funds on party and trade union functions because all this time is registered for everyone as working hours. So how will it be now, with the possibility of the emergence of new parties? Should we all sit at different meetings during our shifts? Or will this remain the communist privilege? I think that working hours must be set aside only for work.

V. Komin, Kaluga region.

I would like to dispute the statement that the 'party does not receive any State subsidies and all its costs are covered using its own resources'. According to the USSR Ministry of Defence decree no. 200, 1984, chapter II, 'Military transport paid for by the Ministry of Defence', point 21, 'Military transport documents for the purposes of official trips are given to the following: e) delegates to CPSU and Communist Youth League (Komsomol) congresses; delegates to CC CPSU and CC Communist Youth League Plenary Sessions, the Central Committee of the Communist Party and the Central Committees of the Communist Youth League in the individual republics, districts, regions and cities; delegates to conferences in district, regional, city and borough Communist party and Komsomol organizations; delegates to party and Komsomol conferences and meetings held in the Soviet Army and Navy; to seminars, elections of party and Komsomol secretaries and to seminars (meetings) on Marxist–Leninist themes as part of the party education programme; to party commission meetings (members of such commissions); to party and Komsomol meetings held away from their usual venues; h) to military personnel engaged on urgent military business; to recruits, warrant officers, female military personnel, manual workers, office workers who need to travel to receive their party and Komsomol documents; to be put on to or taken off party and Komsomol rolls; for the purposes of carrying out various party and Komsomol work – when called upon by party and Komsomol bodies in the Soviet Armed Forces and Navy.'

We think that the rules are the same for other ministries and departments. One can just imagine the cost of all these things, cost which is not paid by the party out of its own funds, but is paid by the Soviet taxpayer.

M, Pavlov, military officer, Kirgizia.

WHEN you read reports in the newspapers about Soviet leaders visiting foreign countries, their names are usually preceded by their position in the party, then their government post, for instance, member of the Politburo CC CPSU [*Central Committee of the Communist party of the Soviet Union*], Foreign Minister Eduard Sheverdnadze. In my opinion we should omit the first part, since when our politicians go on visits abroad, especially to capitalist countries for business talks, they are representing the USSR and not the Communist party. After all, when foreign politicians visit the Soviet Union we hardly ever get given all this sort of information about them.

V. Osakov, Kiev.

I was very upset to read in *AIF* about the political platform of the party formed by Nikolai Travkin.

There is no way I can understand why a plant's personnel should have to buy out fixed assets that were actually purchased with their money. At my plant, for instance, sixty kopecks are deducted from every rouble paid into what's known as the Production Development Fund which is used to build or acquire fixed assets, while only 14.5 kopecks go into the Workers' Incentive Fund.

What this means is that we are having to buy what we have already paid for, and there is no indication as to whom we will be buying it from or where we are supposed to get the money.

Meanwhile, a co-operative has been set up at my plant that uses all the facilities available here, such as the workshops, equipment, electricity, water, heating, etc. The co-operative has not even used up the loan it took out to get started, nor has it had to use its Development Fund into which it paid ten per cent of its profits, leaving the remaining 90 per cent for its members' wages.

192

After the co-operative was closed the Development Fund was distributed among the members.

It appears that the new laws are in no way geared to bringing socialism any closer.

I believe that the following decisions should be taken:

1. Fixed assets paid for from the plant's development funds shall be made the property of the plant's personnel.

2. Upon closure of co-operatives that have been formed at the plant, that have not made use of bank loans and have not set up production facilities using their own development funds, such co-operation shall hand over these development funds in their entirety to the host plant.

R. Lameiko, chief accountant at a plant in Osipovichi,
Mogilev region.

WE have been criticizing Stalin. Brezhnev, Chernenko. Khrushchev and Andropov have also come in for their fair share of barbs. There are people who have even attacked Lenin, the holy of holies. I have my own opinion on all these matters. But then that is not what I want to talk about at the moment!

How are we young people supposed to shape our judgements? You can't find a single book by Stalin in the libraries. True, the guy may not have actually written anything himself, but still ... I think I would be in a better position to understand the epoch and the man himself. I am aware that the people who were purged under Stalin cannot be returned and that the collectivization drive cannot be undone, nor its consequences be rectified. But this is our history, and I want to know it from A to Z ...

Where should I go to read *Malaya Zemlya, Virgin Land Upturned* and other books supposedly written by Brezhnev? Or where can I get Khrushchev's address to the twentieth Party Congress [*the first internal denunciation of Stalin*] without the cuts that were made in it later? Why hasn't the USSR published all Lenin's works yet? And this with perestroika in its fifth year?

I believe that my suggestion that every library should have these above books should be seriously considered. I know that some people will oppose it. But I feel I must repeat that this is our history. It may contain a lot of sorrowful pages, but they cannot be simply burned or crossed out from human memory.

Lena Yurova, seventeen years, Usman, Lipetsk region.

THE school of military chefs where I was employed is one of the exhibition pieces in our military district. It is the first place where high-ranking visitors and commissions are taken when they come to visit the district.

The school is being run in strict accordance with army standards, which apply to both the facilities and discipline. Even so, every time a visitor is expected we all have to jump to and work extra fast. Ceilings have to be whitewashed and walls painted, and all kinds of other things done in haste. No one will say 'Come and see us any time' because people in the Soviet armed forces have got used to impressing visitors with a good layer of gloss.

Students at the school of military chefs are assigned to work at various military and civilian organizations instead of learning the trade. In the morning, the school looks a lot like a labour exchange with teams of students being sent to many different places to do anything but study. Small wonder the graduates' skills leave a lot to be desired.

Now, while so-called aid to other military units is something that can be excused, soldiers being sent to work at civilian organizations is a nonsense. A furniture-making plant 'pays' the school in reject products. It won't be long before the lavatories will be finished in polished wood . . .!

I would like to ask V. Marchenkov who is the commander of the school and a member of the Soviet Communist party, how the pharmaceutical stores, the packaging shop, the commodities/purchases warehouse settle their accounts with the school, and whose pockets the money ends up in?

When I had realized what was happening in the armed forces and that there would be no changes for the better in the immediate future, I decided to leave. I therefore have no fear that I may be prosecuted for my 'unorthodox thinking' and I am convinced that my views are shared by thousands upon thousands of officers and NCOs who have been completely worn out by having to stage showcases. Hopefully, my letter will prompt someone at the top of the military hierarchy to ask himself whether it is preferable to have combat training or 'labour exchanges' in anticipation of yet another inspecting commission.

Y. Kuznetsov, Novosibirsk.

I have been a party member for over forty-five years, and I feel very strongly about people's attitudes to the party. With the heated debate [*on the role of the party*] under way, it is very important to ensure that the top layers of the party hierarchy contain no besmirched reputations.

When Leningrad was busy discussing who had sanctioned the notorious letter by Nina Andreeva [*a Stalinist call for a return to tradition*], someone mentioned the name of Yegor Ligachev, Politburo member and Secretary of the CPSU Central Committee. His name came up again when efforts were being made to find out who was responsible for the tragic decision to use the armed forces in Tbilisi.

The Congress of People's Deputies discussed whether or not Ligachev had taken bribes. It was never proven that Ligachev was corrupt but the very fact of the discussion and his name being linked with such scandals should have prompted him to resign. There's still time before it is too late.

A. Simonovich, Leningrad.

WHEN the Press first started covering Politburo sessions there was some mild interest in them. The reports have since become clichéd and predictable. They always revert to the same old clichés, 'the Politburo discussed and approved this and that, heard and discussed the results of talks, meetings or visits, etc.' Or something like this: 'the Politburo noted with satisfaction the following information.'

The reports never say anything about the discussions or whether there were any other opinions put forward apart from those approved. It's as if everything had passed without the slightest hitch. What is there in this sort of reporting for the reader? The Press should concentrate on important issues, not the trivia.

A. Cherkassov, Perm.

I consider it necessary to supplement the Law of the Union of Soviet Socialist Republics 'On the Procedure for Handling Questions of Secession of a Union Republic from the USSR' with the following article:

In the event of certain circles in a republic which is seceding from the USSR instigating trouble (demonstrations, political meetings, strikes, etc.), which cause material losses, and such disturbances taking place in the period prior to secession from the USSR or during discussion of this question, all losses, in monetary form, from all enterprises maintaining economic ties with the republic in question and losses incurred by national level enterprises situated on the territory of such a republic, shall be compensated for by the republic before it shall secede from the USSR.

N. Kolodyzhii, engineer, Mednogorsk, Orenburg region.

THERE is only one candidate standing in constituency no. 152 of Voronezh district, and that is the first secretary of the district party committee, Mr Kabassik. Although I am not personally acquainted with him, I am pretty sure that I know what sort of people's representative he will be. I formed my opinion on this point after reading the article in *Pravda* entitled 'If Only I Could Be a Leader'. Apparently the *Pravda* journalist went to the district party committee where he was given a list of the best leasing collectives out of the 1,400 in this area. It turned out that not a single one of them existed except on paper. Is it possible that the secretary of the district committee was ignorant of this? And if so, then what sort of secretary is he?

Not long ago I bumped into an old friend of mine on the bus from Voronezh to Boguchar. He was on his way to Voronezh for a television programme. He proudly told me how he had been at a meeting of lessors and had sat in the front row right opposite members of government. One can understand his absolute delight – after all, it is not give to all of us to sit right opposite people from the government, is it?

So I asked him how it was that he came to be at a meeting of lessors. After a bit of humming and hawing he told me that the brigade he worked in had the highest wages of any of the mechanized brigades. His innate honesty would not let him actually go as far as calling himself a lessor. The local leaders who had sent him to the meeting in the first place didn't seem to have any such qualms, nor did our respected candidate to the Congress of People's Deputies who had also been present.

Won't his election to the Congress just be paving the way for more of the same?

Egorova.

PLURALISM is the fashion. But what does this mean? It means that no sooner does an unexpected, out of the ordinary, unorthodox opinion appear, than the heavens thunder and send down lightning flashes of displeasure.

Take Sakharov's much attacked interview on the TV programme *Views*. There was a bit of everything, there was 'critical evaluation', 'discussion and opinion forming', 'proper conclusions' and 'selection procedures' . . . Dreadful terminology! Thank God the roads to the Lubyanka and the psychiatric hospitals have been closed off!

So what really happened? This man, who is without a doubt an actor of some quality, publicly and honestly stated his opinion and produced arguments to support it on a rather precarious subject. What if Mr Sakharov is wrong, or he has chosen the wrong time, or he has misunderstood something, let something slip? This is his opinion and nobody has the right to, and indeed cannot, deprive him of his opinion. One may well not agree with him, one can argue and try to show him that he is wrong. But one must do all of this democratically, exercising every due care to make sure that people have the right to be different, and one must be careful not to fall into the trap of saying 'How can he say such things on Soviet TV – it's supposed to be State-, party-run!' or 'I forbid it!' or 'I'll put a stop to this!', which, as we saw recently, is still all too easy to do.

This is what we should be afraid of rather than the opinion of an honest and courageous man who believes that the word 'government' should be synonymous with 'legally based', and the word 'party' with 'Leninism'.

A. M. Barenboim, war and labour veteran, teacher
member of Communist party since 1942.

YOUR recent article called 'Three Figures' simply astonished me. It was the one about the human losses in Russia after the 1917 October Revolution. My God, how awful! One hundred and ten million, seven hundred thousand people! That's half the country! It is only now that one realizes the price to be paid for mad experiments. And the worst thing is that the criminal responsible for creating all those hecatombs, who for decades added to those enormous, unbelievable mountains of bodies, is still to this day alive and free. Not only that, but the murderer is doing very well thank you, and continuing to conduct its cruel experiments (which are no more than cynical fun at the expense of whole nations and peoples).

This monster, this criminal, is none other than the Communist party of the Soviet Union! I am afraid that I can no longer hear the words 'communist' and 'communism' without a shudder of fear. It's like a knot of venomous snakes. And still they are using the mass media to spread their views and to talk, talk, talk . . .

All these secretaries, political information officers, party organizers, and party bodies – it's amazing their tongues don't dry up! Yet they don't seem to feel the tiniest little bit of remorse for what they have done to the Russian people, for the fact that they have turned the country into a stinking cesspit! And still they carry on giving their opinions and calling upon people to do things. It's beyond belief! It's monstrous! And I would like to know if anyone would be amoral enough to stand up in a court and defend Stalin (although who knows, maybe there is someone who would do it just in case). And is there any noble soul in our country who would stand up in court and defend the Russian people from the Communist party? Who would bring this criminal organization to justice for genocide against Russians and other nations? What else would you call the murder of 110,700,000 people?

S. Alekseev, Perm.

(*The article in question was by Soviet émigré writer I. Kurganov and examined the impact of the upheavals in the USSR between 1917 and 1959, particularly the loss of life in the Revolution, the Civil War, World War II and the Stalin purges. Kurganov took known figures on deaths and added in statistics on what natural growth should have been in the period and came up with the figure of over 110 million casualties of the wars, external and internal – Ed.)*

AS I said in the interview published in *AIF* last January, I am not afraid of 'standing out from the crowd'.

I feel I need to explain what I mean, so that people don't get the impression that I and other political émigrés have been to all intents and purposes 'forgiven' and 'given permission' to return home.

This couldn't be further from the truth. I think that the government should invite political émigrés to come home. It should invite those who, not only have not done anything anti-constitutional, but who, on the contrary, during the period of stagnation spoke out for the same things that the leading edge in perestroika is now demanding. And what's more, the government should apologize to them for what the previous government did to them, and compensate them for damage done. All these political émigrés should be given back their Soviet citizenship.

Instead of which the re-emigration problem is only being partially dealt with. Recently Rostropovich and his wife had their Soviet passports returned. While this is only to be welcomed, why stop at them? Rostropovich demanded that Solzhenitsyn should also be given back his Soviet passport. But again – why stop at Solzhenitsyn?

There should be some basic principle governing policy on this question: either reinstate as citizens all who lost their Soviet passports as a punishment for daring to hold different views, or don't reinstate anyone at all. This is the whole essence of a legally based State – there cannot be one law for some and another for the rest.

I would go further and say that Soviet citizenship should be given back not only to those who had it taken away by the Praesidium of the Supreme Soviet, but also to those who due to political persecution were forced to leave on an 'Israeli visa' (which the KGB used to insist on) just to avoid yet again ending up in prison.

In addition they should be allocated homes, offered jobs, and those who were already retired at the time of exile should be paid their pensions for the full period of enforced emigration (incidentally, all other States, with the exception of ours, send pensions to their retired citizens no matter which country they have elected to live in).

Since these questions have yet to be resolved, none of the political émigrés of whom I know are yet able to return to the Soviet Union.

P. Abovin-Egides, Paris.

MY son, a student, was recently discharged from the armed forces. He served in Mongolia and it took him six days to get home. The command provided him with R20, documents for his return trip via train (in a sitting car) and dry rations. He paid R15 extra to travel in a sleeping car and arrived in Belgorod. A bus ticket from Belgorod to our town costs R4, but my son bought soft drinks en route and did not have enough money for the bus ticket.

Fortunately for him the driver said: 'Come in old buddy! I had a similar experience when returning from the army.' My son did not have to pay him a single kopeck. I thank the driver and all those who help soldiers en route, offering them tea, food and other things. But why does the Defence Ministry shift the responsibility on to other people? It does not grudge the expenses on air tickets for recruits. But no care is taken of the demobilized.

People say time and again that not everything is all right in our armed forces. What we need is a law to guarantee the defence of young soldiers' human dignity.

Z. Molchanova Alexeyvka, Belgorod region.

IN September last year workers at the Yuzhnobugsky State farm in Nikolayev region came across an ammunition dump: several dozen large-calibre shells and anti-tank rockets hidden in a straw sack. The weapons could only have come from a nearby testing range in the Odessa military district and were evidently destined for well-known areas of unrest.

Interestingly, representatives of military units invited to the scene flatly refused to acknowledge the weapons as theirs. People still do not know where the rockets and ammunition came from. It looks like the military leadership are not particularly keen to let people know of such facts and how weapons are kept and taken stock of in the army. Through *AIF* I want to put this question to Marshal Yazov: How come the extremists in various parts of the country have thousands of firearms, rockets etc. at their disposal?

A. Yepifanov, Nikolayev.

Question and Answer

Workers at the Moscow Khrunichev plant put questions to KGB officers about their role.

Q. *How many foreign secret service agents have the KGB apprehended recently?*

A. In the past few years the KGB has rendered harmless thirty foreign agents and has found many listening devices in Soviet establishments abroad. We are also fighting those who sell our commercial secrets to foreign organizations. For example, this year we have arrested a man called Lukashevich, a former employee of the Ministry of Industrial Building Materials, who was bribed by foreign companies to supply them with secret information.

Q. *What technologies are being used by Western countries against the Soviet Union?*

A. There are about forty spy satellites over the Soviet Union; six of them intercept information from Soviet radio relay devices. About 2,000 foreign observation stations are situated along the Soviet border and foreign aircraft make reconnaissance flights over the western borders and over the eastern borders of the Soviet Union.

Western space reconnaissance can detect objects that are no more than 1.5 metres across on Soviet territory. We have proved that Western secret services are using technical means of espionage on the territory of the country. According to

American sources the US spends some $20 billion on technological espionage.

Q. *Is the KGB involved in the rehabilitation of Stalin's victims?*

A. Yes, and actively. In 1988 and the first quarter of 1989 we rehabilitated 47,088 people and refused rehabilitation to 3,492 former members of punitive units, members of gangs and nationalist units of the German Army, falsifiers of cases, etc. At present there are no officers who have been responsible for persecutions of the Stalinist period. [*In August 1990 Gorbachev gave blanket rehabilitation to the victims of the purges – Ed.*]

Organized crime has stepped up of late, how is the KGB helping to combat it?

A. The KGB takes a direct part in combating organized crime and racketeering. We work in close contact with the militia, the procurator's offices and other law enforcement bodies. The KGB also tackles cases of attempted assassinations.

Q. *Will the KGB give its HQ on Dzerzhinskaya Square to a child care institution?*

A. The question was answered by V. Kryuchov when he was appointed KGB chairman. The issue should be regarded from the economic viewpoint. Will the State budget gain from this transfer? To move to another building for the KGB would mean transferring all communications, technical services and auxiliary devices, which will call for major outlays. The KGB has no special claims on the building; the issue should be regarded not emotionally but soberly with a view to State interests.

EPILOGUE

The political topography of the Soviet Union seems to be changing daily. The contours alter in the wake of the last hot storm of rhetoric, rearrange into new patterns in the eddies and vacuums. I keep asking 'what is going to happen?' Lots of answers, all different, none good. Hope abandoned in favour of certainty?

'Oh, there will be a military *coup*. But it won't succeed. Nothing succeeds here. It is our destiny.' This is told to me in an 'Indian' restaurant with only tea and a few cheese sandwiches on the menu. Perhaps my unintended slapstick broke the reserve: the stool I sat on collapsed under me, spilling me among the dirt and crumbs. Everyone clapped, and laughed. 'This is our life . . . join it,' someone said.

This is a life, a society, you can ridicule in raucous goodwill, but can't insult or defile. No one believes in any of it. Well, not the majority, anyway.

A day or two later, unwittingly, I discovered the other view. Haltingly, politely, I asked an old attendant for a towel in a lavatory. He boomed: 'Of course. Our great leader taught us never to refuse a request.' I smiled. I should have known better from the list to port caused by the medals on his chest. Stalin? 'Refusal was terminal, wasn't it?' thinking I was joining in the joke. He launched into a tirade and almost had to be restrained from slapping the insolent disbelief off my face.

The country needs a strong leader, a *vozhd*!

Is there a Soviet Union any more? Fourteen of the fifteen

republics have declared for some kind of independence. I watched a Press conference with President Gorbachev on the day he was awarded the Nobel Prize. 'Second prize,' someone muttered. 'Lost the Cold War, won the Peace Prize.' It's difficult not to think that here is an unelected leader attempting to govern a country that no longer exists, or that coercion kept the country cohesive. 'We will take our freedom,' in a famous Russian maxim, 'when we are ordered to take it.' Maybe now it should be, 'when not ordered not to'.

Mikhail Sergelvich Gorbachev, history will surely record, was one of the greatest of men. Is he to be exiled from his country's future? This is the country of exile, as the previous pages witness.

I have been living in a friend's flat, as near to reality as a foreign passport and a return ticket allow. Reality is: nothing is for sale, but everything is buyable, either for foreign currency or American cigarettes. It's Marlboro country, the new frontier. From caviare, rare icons, gold and jewels, to influence, privilege and physical harm, it all has a dollar availability.

What will happen? Something better than now, certainly. What do I know? Journalists have the camouflage of tomorrow's chip papers, historians the disguise of time. Do they get it right?

The latest topical joke is that Boris Yeltsin has amended the 500-day economic programme to two days: 'On day one we declare war on Sweden.' And? 'On day two we surrender, of course.'

Laughable. The huge memorial iron tank barriers, crosses, a mortar's range from the centre of Moscow, mark the point where the war turned, where the Soviets refused to surrender even with more than twenty million dead, and fascism fled.

So, to the past, to the hospitality and friendship, to the future of this great country, or countries.

INDEX